D0350278

Jihyun Park was born in Chongjin, North Korea, in 1968. She experienced acute poverty, famine, illness, and intimidation. She first escaped at the age of 29. After her second escape from North Korea, with the help of the UN, she was granted asylum seeker status in 2008 and moved to Bury, Greater Manchester, where she lives with her husband Kwang and three children. She has been outreach and project officer at the European Alliance for Human Rights in North Korea and is an online language tutor and human rights activist.

Seh-lynn Chai is South Korean. She divides her time between London, where she lives with her family, and Seoul, where her parents reside. She has a Bachelor's and a Master's degree in French Literature from L'Université Paris-Sorbonne (Paris IV) and an MBA from Columbia Business School. After a career in Finance at JP Morgan, she is now an active campaigner for peace on the Korean Peninsula and for human rights and has served on the Korean government's Peaceful Unification Advisory Council (PUAC).

THE HARD ROAD OUT

ONE WOMAN'S ESCAPE FROM NORTH KOREA

JIHYUN PARK
AND SEH-LYNN CHAI

HarperNorth
Windmill Green,
Mount Street,
Manchester, M2 3NX

A division of
HarperCollins*Publishers*
1 London Bridge Street
London SE1 9GF

www.harpercollins.co.uk

HarperCollins*Publishers*
1st Floor, Watermarque Building, Ringsend Road
Dublin 4, Ireland

First published in English by HarperNorth in 2022

3 5 7 9 10 8 6 4 2

Translated by Sarah Baldwin-Beneich

Jihyun Park and Seh-lynn Chai assert the moral right to
be identified as the co-authors of this work

A catalogue record for this book
is available from the British Library

HB ISBN: 978-0-00-854140-8
TPB ISBN: 978-0-00-854141-5

Printed and bound in the UK using 100% renewable electricity at
CPI Group (UK) Ltd

To my husband and children, and to the brave citizens of North Korea.

Jihyun Park

To Soojin and Jimin, for the humanity and light they have in them; to Charles, who believed in me when I did not.

Seh-lynn Chai

PROLOGUE

Jihyun's story could be my own. She is my age, speaks my language, loves kimchi, and is Korean. She fled to China to escape a dictatorship and protect her family before seeking asylum in Britain some ten years ago. I came to London around the same time when my husband's job brought us here, and I've been here ever since. I haven't swum across the Tumen River or faced down the Gobi Desert like Jihyun has, but I have crossed many borders in my time. And each time, like a tortoise with its shell, I have carried my 'home' – that is, my Korean identity – with me from one country to the next. Jihyun is from the North and I am from the South, but we share a single identity: we are both Korean. And that is what saves us.

Jihyun speaks of her childhood, her family, prison camps, slavery and escape. I write of my need to connect two lives, to create a link, to repair: who would she and I have become, had our country not been divided?

Writing brings us together. As Jihyun tells me about her life in North Korea, I take on her perspective, I access her inner world. I become her. Our experiences are not the same, but childhood, death, suffering and dreams … these we share.

Jihyun and I meet for the first time in 2014, in Manchester, during the filming of a documentary by Amnesty International. An interpreter friend of mine has to back out at the last minute and asks me to stand in for her. The job is to interview Jihyun in Korean and transcribe her answers in English for the short film, *The Other Interview*, which is scheduled to come out soon. I am nervous – not only because I'm not a professional interpreter, but also because the idea of speaking to a North Korean makes me uneasy. Isn't that risky? Am I allowed to engage with a North Korean citizen? What if somebody reports me to the Embassy of South Korea in London for spying? I am still mulling over these questions as I fill out the paperwork for Amnesty International. Driven by some unnamed feeling, I accept the job. In the car carrying the Amnesty team from London to Manchester, the director brings me up to speed on the project. But the movie in my head is an entirely different one.

I picture my childhood bedroom in our apartment in Seoul. On the wall is a poster showing a fist against a bright-red background, with the words 'Down with Communists' in big letters above it. The poster won me second prize in the anti-communism poster competition organised by my primary school. It's signed and dated 'Seh-lynn, 1976'. I hear the shrill sound of the sirens that signal, on the fifteenth of every month, the start of the simulated attack – a practice established in 1953, at the end of the Korean War. During the simulation, life stops. No more cars in the streets. No more children in the schoolyards. People in their homes hurriedly descend to the bomb shelter in the basement of their apartment building. Seoul becomes a ghost town. Then, twenty minutes later, life begins again as though nothing has happened. And the fifteenth of the following month, the same sirens and helicopters, the same deserted streets. It's a routine like any other.

***

As the child of a diplomat, I was keenly aware of the presence of that 'other' Korea. When we lived in Africa for instance, when I was twelve, there were three or four South Korean families in the city where we lived, all there on diplomatic posts, and there were probably as many if not fewer North Korean families. They were hard to spot, except for the occasional glimpse in the supermarket, because they rarely came out of their homes. When they did, it was always in a group.

It was the first time in my life I'd seen North Koreans, but despite our proximity the boundaries separating us remained absolute. Under no circumstances were we to talk to them. I was to hold tight to my mother's arm and stay close to the shopping cart lest I be kidnapped. When our cars passed in the street, I would scowl at them. They scared me, but at least I felt safe behind the glass where they couldn't get me. These encounters never lasted more than a few seconds, but those seconds marked me. I had been raised to believe all North Koreans were the enemy, and here we were, suddenly face to face.

Other than that, though, being Korean in Africa was brilliant. With my slanted eyes and straight black hair, some people thought I was a cousin of Bruce Lee or Jackie Chan, while others saw me as representing the country of economic miracle, South Korea. At home, the Korean flag was always flying. I dreamed of becoming my country's president. Most of my foreign friends didn't know the difference between North and South Korea, and in some ways that was fine with me. It meant I didn't have to explain that the North was communist and the South capitalist, especially since I didn't understand how that had come about and found it all very complicated. I was simply Korean, but in my mind being Korean meant being *South* Korean. In 'my' Korea there were no North Koreans. In 1979, the year I turned fourteen, my parents announced that President Park Chung-hee had been assassinated by a North Korean spy. My mother wept. I felt sad without really knowing why. It was the beginning of my historical awareness.

***

The interview gets under way. It's the first time I've ever found myself face to face with a North Korean. Roughly my age, her face is very peaceful, and like me she is wearing glasses. She looks 'normal', not 'evil'. But I am terrified. What if she calls me a capitalist pig? Or worse, what if I am the one who says something terrible? My years of being raised to distrust North Koreans have left me with ingrained beliefs that I haven't ever really questioned.

It is a good thing the cameraman from Amnesty interrupts the interview to adjust the microphone on her blouse and the position of her chair. Jihyun is polite and smiles but she does not give me a good eye contact.

Little by little, her story grabs me. My initial fear turns to shock, especially when she rolls up the bottom of her black pants and shows me the scar on her leg from her time in prison camp. My eyes fill with tears, my vision blurs, but I catch every word, every emotion, every subtle shade of meaning and tone. At the end of the interview I'm exhausted but strangely satisfied, even relieved. I have won a battle against my own beliefs about North Koreans, managed to favour the human over the political. I have just met one of those who never get talked about in political circles, one of those who reveal the history of a human soul, and generally get omitted by the big picture of History – it's a small gift that has come to me out of nowhere.

My path crosses Jihyun's several more times at human rights conferences in London, and even if we are always very happy to see each other again we remain somewhat restrained. We keep it professional. Our meetings alter my perspective on the fate of our divided country, at least intellectually. We have, each in our own way, from either side of the border – she to the North and I to the South – been simulating war for almost fifty years. I have been her enemy and she has been mine. 'We' were the good guys and 'they' were the bad guys – and vice versa. What a coup on the part of the world powers, turning us against each other. We have become our own enemies. One question leads to another. I can't stop wondering: where have 5,000 years of shared history gone?

My point of view continues to develop over the two years that follow the interview in Manchester, until it becomes urgent for me to face this question of fundamental identity. Was two years also needed for trust to grow between Jihyun and me?

Jihyun had been mentioning that she wanted to leave a testimony for her children, until one day she asks *me* if I would write her story. *Me*? Didn't she already have a Canadian writer in mind? She wants it to be written by a Korean – without the go-between of a translator – who can articulate emotions she can't express in any other language. She wants to use words that will bring her truth to life without eliciting either judgement or misunderstandings lost in translation. She wants to touch people's souls – yours and mine. She wants to tell the story of an ordinary North Korean family and the extraordinary suffering they underwent. *With me*. Reaching this point, both of us wishing to share our stories, has been anything but easy.

And I accept. I want to give voice to history's invisible people – a people torn apart, a people no one talks about. I want to be among those who begin to talk, those who seek to leave behind the suffering brought on by a painful and tragic disunion that has been in place since the end of the Second World War. When I speak about Jihyun, people around me are interested. I want to tell the story of her battle to save the lives of other human beings, as well as the story of the Korean Peninsula shrouded in amnesia: forty years of Japanese occupation, followed by a fratricidal conflict – the so-called Korean War – and a state of denial over the separation of the country ever since. Whatever it takes, we must lift the veil that covers up this chaotic past. We must tell it like it is. We *must* write this book.

We hope it will be an initial step towards undoing seventy years of forced isolation on both sides of the border. Yes, Jihyun lived under a communist regime and I in a democracy; yes, she was forced to leave her country and cannot return, while I left mine voluntarily and can go back when I choose. But the threat of war looms over the peninsula more than ever, and we no longer have time to focus on the differences that separate us.

This is Jihyun's story, but it is mine as well. I ignored the 'monster from the North' for as long as I could, keeping it at bay until I couldn't hide from it any more. It became too big, too familiar. Or too *unfamiliar*. Korea is about more than Gangnam Style in the South and nuclear tests in the North. Between these clichés lives a whole world of ordinary people like us. It took me some time to accept that North Korea was part of my country – I'd been afraid of it for so long – but recent events have left me no choice. *Don't spit on your own face*, as the Korean proverb goes. North Korean, South Korean … we are all, first and foremost, Koreans. This book might have been written in two voices, but in the end both 'I's became the voice of a single restored identity – this is one story, of one Korea.

Seh-lynn Chai, London 2022

CHAPTER ONE

'Mummy, why did you abandon me?'

One afternoon in 2012, sitting beside me on a bench in a Manchester park, Chul asks me the question. I search for an answer but can't find one. Where to begin? What does he remember? Chul was very young when I left him in China to save him from going to prison in North Korea. But I did go back to get him a year later, and since then I have obtained asylum for him in England. Today, here we are, safe and sound. And happy.

We *are* happy, aren't we?

While these questions swirl in my head like leaves in a gale, the word 'abandon' sparks fear inside me: my heart races, I'm flooded with guilt. I realise that this question has just breached a world I've created out of things unsaid, a world whose apparent calm was merely a façade, a precarious world in which I'd overcome the pain of the past by covering it up. My heart aches at the thought that Chul hasn't dared to ask this question since 2004, the moment of our separation. My eyes fill with tears. To think that he has endured eight years of silence, eight years during which he has preferred to keep everything to himself, crushes me with pain. I can't keep covering up the past. I must tell my son why I can't simply say, 'I didn't abandon you.' I must tell him why I can't find the words, why no sound will come from my throat.

I must tell him my story.

***

The distant past comes back to me like a murky dream, a lost world that collapsed before my eyes, swallowing up the people and places that had been most dear to me. The place I will never go back to again is Chongjin, a city in North Hamgyong Province on the east coast of North Korea.

Chongjin is a rectangular city built on a plain, on one side nestling up against the base of a rocky mountain range and, on the other, looking out over the water that separates Korea from Japan. Koreans call this body of water *Donghae*, or East Sea, while to the Japanese it is the Sea of Japan. Being near the sea made summer's heat bearable, but the winters, when temperatures generally fell below zero, were bitterly cold. It had once been a small fishing village, but given its strategic location between Japan and Manchuria, it turned into a boom town during the Japanese occupation, from 1910 until 1945. By the 1970s, it was a dynamic, thriving industrial port, thanks to the steel and synthetic textile mills built along the coast. Japan and the Soviet Union had chosen the city as their preferred trade partner, and with a population of more than 500,000, it had fast become the third-largest city in North Korea.

I can still see myself as a little girl of four in a tiny, 16-square-metre apartment in a suburb to the south of the city, in a district called Ranam. At the time, Ranam was known both for its chicken farms and for its newly built housing for Chongjin's factory workers.

My father, Park Seong-il, was a tractor-excavator operator. My mother, Ro Eun-sook, had worked in the same factory as him, but after they married she chose to become an *ajumma*, or housewife; North Korean law allowed her to stay home, and she took advantage of it. My father had spotted her early on, not long after she'd started working at the factory. She drove a small forklift with gusto, and seeing that, he said to himself she'd be the perfect wife for him. He had an elderly mother, two younger brothers and a sister to take care of: he needed a hard-working, devoted wife. He just had to keep her identity a secret from his mother, since he knew she would not approve of a future daughter-in-law who was not a member of the *Chosun Rodongdang*, or Korean Workers' Party, and who was therefore a member of the lower class.

When I was born, my older sister, Myeong-sil, wasn't around. My parents vaguely explained that she had gone to live with my grandmother, and I didn't ask questions. My brother, Jeong-ho, was not born yet, so at the time it was just the three of us at home. Our apartment was located on the fourth floor of a faded red-brick building. There were ten apartments per floor and they were all numbered; those with even numbers had only one room, while odd-numbered apartments contained two. Ours, which had been assigned to my parents when they were married, was number 4. It was located at the end of the hallway, next to the door that led to the roof, which I was forbidden to open. The buildings were named according to where the residents worked, such as 'Steelworks' or 'Shipyard'. Ours was called 'Mechanical Department No. 2' after the car factory where my father serviced cars. Everyone worked at the same place, everyone lived in the same lodging, everyone earned the same amount of money. It was 'the Workers' Paradise'. Each building represented an *Inminban* – *inmin* meaning people, and *ban* meaning class. It wasn't surprising that the word *inmin* appeared so often in everyday language: everything belonged to the group, nothing to the individual. In the entryway of the building there was a glass-enclosed booth where the building manager, or *Inminbanjang*, was on duty. That position was held by one of the female residents, usually an *ajumma*. I remember Mrs Choi, our *Inminbanjang*, very well. She was the most important woman in the building: a member of the Party, she embodied *Juche*, the ideology of self-reliance developed by North Korea founder Kim Il-sung in the 1960s. About thirty, she terrorised the building with her booming voice. She was the type of cold, authoritarian woman who ordered everyone around and was always in control. Mrs Choi had a whole network of agents – usually the building's vulnerable inhabitants – who spied on the other residents.

She gathered information, then passed it directly to the Department of National Security.

Facing the glass booth was a large bulletin board covered with handwritten announcements about cleaning crew rotas and air raid drills. The Americans, you see, might attack at any moment, and drills had become a daily occurrence. In the evening, vehicles fitted with loudspeakers drove around on patrol to ensure that all the lights were out. At the faintest glimmer, the loudspeakers would blare, '*Apartment 3, lights out!*' If you were unlucky enough to be the culprit, you were doomed: the authorities would cut the electricity in all three buildings as a collective punishment, and you would be cursed by your neighbours to the end of your days.

The staircase that led to our apartment was at the end of the hallway. Was it ever clean? As a little girl, I watched my mom energetically wash and scrub the steps; the following day, it was my neighbour's mum's turn. Thanks to all the scouring, that staircase became more dazzling every day. The inside of our apartment was whitewashed. As in all Korean homes, a shoe cabinet sat just inside the door. The only room was straight ahead, with a window overlooking the street. To the right was the kitchen, and to the left a small toilet cubicle. There was no flush, so we had to add water by hand. For washing up, there was a water bucket, a small bar of foul-smelling soap, and salt. There was never enough toothpaste for all of us, so very early on I got in the habit of dipping my finger in the salt and rubbing it on my teeth to clean them.

Past the toilet was the one room. There was nothing in it but a wooden cupboard containing blankets and clothes – one of the only pieces of furniture in our home. In keeping with Korean tradition, we all slept on the floor. It was covered with linoleum and was warmed underneath by hot air from the wood stove, a typical Korean heating system known as *Ondol*. At night, we would take our quilted cotton mats out of the wardrobe and open them out on the floor. The next day, we would carefully fold them up again and put them back in the cupboard. There was one blanket for the three of us. This was how the typical North Korean family lived.

In the evening, the room was lit by a single bare bulb hanging from the ceiling. You had to be careful; light bulbs were rare, a gift of Kim Il-sung, and not available to everyone. They were rationed, so people burned candles to conserve their bulb. We lived in the dark most of the time and spoke little, since the apartment walls were paper-thin. There is a Korean proverb that says, 'Words in the day are heard by birds; words at night are heard by mice.' And then there was the picture, framed in pale wood that hung on the wall facing the wardrobe. It spoke to me, watched me, heard me; it even read my mind. This was The Portrait. The Portrait had a beautiful smile and a kind air. *Eomeoni* – which is what I called my mother – and *Abeoji* – my father – carefully cleaned The Portrait every day with a special cloth. They took great care of our beloved father, Kim Il-sung.

I was born on 30 July 1968, but in North Korea we don't celebrate children's birthdays. Only the birthday of Kim Il-sung, on 15 April, is celebrated. But every 30 July, I was entitled to a bowl of rice, and it was a huge luxury not to have to share it. A big bowl of rice, just for me: now, *that* was a gift!

Even though *Eomeoni* was an *ajumma*, she didn't have time to play with me. The mothers in the building were also responsible for keeping the walls gleaming white, and they spent their time whitewashing them. They may have been housewives, but they were never really home. They were always out, cleaning the stairwells, the streets, the buildings. We children played by ourselves in a sandlot that must have been there since the building was built in the sixties. Much of the housing had been created for soldiers completing their military service and who were going to work in the steel mills of Chongjin. The street I lived on was crawling with kids whooping and messing around. Our shoes had holes in them and our toes stuck out, but that didn't keep us from running all over the place and having fun.

These were the kids with whom I learned to play hide-and-seek, catch tadpoles in the river, and pretend to fight the Americans.

***

One day, *Abeoji* announced that I was to go and live with *Halmeoni*, my father's mother. Just as my big sister *Unni* (I never call her by her first name, Myeong-sil, out of respect, since she is my elder sister) had gone to live with *Halmeoni* when she was four; now it was my turn. It did not occur to me to ask why. To the little girl I was, this was normal. Every child in the world went to live with his or her grandmother at the age of four and came home at seven, when they were school age. To prepare me, *Abeoji* warned me that *Halmeoni* was difficult to live with. *OK*, I said to myself, *I'm about to take my first train ride, and for that I can put up with a difficult Halmeoni!* Getting official authorisation to travel to another region was difficult, but after a long wait it finally came, and all that was left was to pack my bag. I remember feeling so happy to be taking a trip with my father for the first time that I left without even saying goodbye to my mother.

***

To get to Pukchong, where *Halmeoni* lived, we travelled south by train along the east coast of Hamgyong Province. The ride lasted three hours. At Pukchong, we took another train to Sin-Pukchong, then walked half an hour to the house *Abeoji* had grown up in until he was fourteen, when he began his military service. By then, *Halmeoni* was a very poor widow. It would mean one less mouth to feed, my father thought as he enlisted, lying about his age. After about ten years with the Jonyon regiment of Kumgangsan, in Kangwondo Province, he was sent to Chongjin, where he operated a red tractor-excavator in the Second Mechanical Division of the car servicing factory – his first and only line of work, the work he would do for the rest of his life.

CHAPTER ONE

The dirt roads leading to *Halmeoni*'s house followed the ups and downs of the mountainous countryside. Everywhere I looked, I saw collective farms. There was very little farm machinery. I didn't hear a single motor. Oxen-pulled carts, or *soorye*, passed by. They were full of corn and Korean cabbage, used to make *Kimchi*, fermented cabbage with salt and chilli powder – the national dish. By the side of the road, a few women were hard at work repairing the roads that had been eroded by the rain, with shovels as their only tools.

Abeoji stopped at last in front of an old, one-storey house situated in the middle of some barren fields at the foot of a dirt-coloured hill. The tiles of the roof came in every shade of grey: the newer ones were coal-dark, while time had turned others greyish-green with mould and still others were the colour of stone. The faded hues signalled the house's age, while the walls, white as chalk, stood out in startling contrast against a desiccated landscape drained of colour.

My grandmother *Halmeoni*, my sister *Unni* and my father's older brother *Keun Abeoji* were waiting for us outside. *Jagueun Aboeji*, the youngest brother, and *Gomo*, his younger sister, were at work and missing that afternoon, as well as my father's other younger brother, who happened to be in the army. Grey-haired, her face and hands wrinkled, *Halmeoni* must have been about sixty. She frightened me: her back made a right angle with the rest of her body, which placed her eyes at the level of my own. Even when she stood, she couldn't straighten up. That day she was wearing a white blouse and a long black skirt. She had the same clear, cutting, authoritarian voice as my father. She was holding *Unni*, my older sister, by the hand.

Thanks to my father's warning, I'd prepared myself for the meeting with my grandmother but it hadn't occurred to me to wonder about my sister. She had come to live with *Halmeoni* three years earlier and was about to return home to our parents and begin school. Taken by surprise, *Unni* and I tried to hide our unease: we were sisters, yes, but so what? What were we supposed to do in this situation? Fortunately, at that moment *Unni* let go of *Halmeoni*. She ran towards me with a big grin and grabbed my hand. Saying nothing, she just smiled at me. I felt reassured – it was good to have an older sister after all.

The inside of the house was bare and dark, but the wooden ceiling made it feel cosy. Compared to the cold, bare walls I was used to in Ranam, the wood seemed luxurious. To find the kitchen, all I had to do was follow the smell of *Doenjang*, or fermented bean soup.

It was a typical Korean kitchen, with a drop-floor and woodstove. The two levels of the kitchen floor made it possible to place a huge metal pot, which served as the stove, on the elevated part. Thanks to this system, you could stand on the lower level and cook at waist height. I remember often being tempted to peek under the lid of the pot – there was always hot rice inside! – but it was too heavy, and I couldn't lift it alone. The hot air from the stove wasn't necessarily distributed evenly, though, and certain parts of the floor were warmer than others, but at least the house was more or less heated.

This initial meeting with my sister was brief. *Abeoji* had to return to Chongjin that same evening to work and he took *Unni* with him. Standing on the threshold, he held *Unni*'s hand, while I held *Halmeoni*'s. *Unni* and I had barely met, and already it was time to say goodbye.

Unni was crying, and I began to cry, too – not out of sorrow, but because I wanted to be like her. *Halmeoni*, on the other hand, was stony-faced. She didn't even give *Unni* a hug. Her Confucian beliefs forbade her from expressing her emotions in public; she had to remain stoic and dignified. Brusquely, she held out a schoolbag and some pencils she'd been clutching the entire time – school supplies she'd bought for her granddaughter. It was as though she wanted by any means to keep this parting short. *Abeoji* made one final, solemn bow to his mother, as though it were the last time he would see her. Then, as *Unni* continued to weep, he took her hand and set off down the road. Once they had gone, *Halmeoni* went to her room and allowed her tears to flow in silence. After a while, she raised her eyes and, seeing that I was in the room, tenderly invited me to sit down next to her.

'*Bae gopah*? (Are you hungry?)' she asked me.

'*Aniyo*. No, *Halmeoni*.'

'*Gueurae, doetda*. (Ah, then all is well.)'

She wanted to be sure I was not crying from hunger. Not being hungry was all that mattered to her.

***

In the rear courtyard was the chestnut tree that gave the place its name. It was customary to name one's house after the child that lives in it, but since there were no children at *Halmeoni*'s, the villagers called it *Bamnamoo Jib*, or 'the house with the chestnut tree'.

'*Halmeoni, Halmeoni*, come look!' I cried one day. 'Hedgehogs!' I pointed to the little globes covered in spikes that lay on the ground in the courtyard. I can still see *Halmeoni*'s ready smile as she explained that these were called chestnuts and we could eat them. I followed her into the kitchen. Before too long I was carried away by the smell of roasting that seeped from the oven and drifted through the house. As I breathed in the smell, I savoured my first taste of roasted chestnut in silence – I wanted to fill myself with this feeling of happiness forever.

At home in Ranam there was never enough to eat, and my stomach was always empty. The bowls of rice (or, more often, corn) that my mother gave me never managed to fill me up. Here, at *Halmeoni*'s, I was spoilt: I had a soft-boiled egg every day for breakfast – I had rarely tasted anything so delicious – and roasted chestnuts for an afternoon snack! With every passing day I became more attached to my grandmother. Despite her looks, she was no longer the wicked witch my father had described. She played hide-and-seek with me, fed me well, and was gentle and affectionate. At night, before going to bed, she would unfold my mat and place it in the warmest corner of the room. By the light of a candle (which she preferred to an electric bulb), she would weave wondrous tales about the sun and the moon. I felt loved.

Halmeoni even let me stay home instead of going to nursery school, which all the village children my age did. Every day I played with my friends – the chickens, a stick, and some rocks. One day, I put my stick to the test by beating to death a passing snake. Back in Ranam, I had played at hitting Americans and South Koreans with my stick. In both cases I was proud of my abilities.

I tried to keep busy, but the truth is, I was lonely. I missed my friends and the hubbub of Ranam. I missed my parents. Travel permits were hard to come by, so I knew they wouldn't visit me. I also knew that their life in Ranam prevented them from leaving the city. *Unni* had gone through this, arriving at *Halmeoni*'s house when she was three and not once seeing our parents during her entire stay. There was no telephone, so we didn't speak to each other. We didn't write each other letters. We didn't visit. That is how it was.

It was completely unexpected, then, that my parents should appear one day, long before they were due.

The night before, I had been awakened by the muffled sound of tears and moans from the room next door:

Aïgo …

It was my aunt *Gomo*. She was weeping.

'*Halmeoni* is dead,' she told me.

Dead?

I took the information back to bed with me without really knowing what it meant. It wasn't until the next morning, when I was sent to have breakfast at the neighbours', that I understood something out of the ordinary was happening. My uncles and aunt looked sombre, and they couldn't stop crying. When I asked why *Halmeoni* wasn't getting up to prepare the meal, nobody bothered to explain it to me. *Gomo* simply sent me outside to play. Later, the neighbours came, carrying a large wooden box, the inside of which was coated with some sort of sticky black paste that gave off a terrible smell. I was fascinated by what was happening. The adults dressed *Halmeoni* in her everyday outfit – black skirt and white shirt – and placed her in this box they called a 'coffin'. I wondered why *Halmeoni*'s body was so limp as they dressed her, lifting her up and laying her back down. The coffin was placed in my great-uncle's room. I managed to sneak only the briefest glimpse before making way for the neighbours who had begun arriving to pay their respects. *Halmeoni* looked forlorn. I loved her so much. What had happened? Why the sadness on her face?

The next day I went outside to play, but *Halmeoni* didn't come with me: she stayed in her box. I saw a yellowish-coloured liquid seeping out of one corner. A revolting stench filled the room, but in spite of the smell the visitors kept coming during the days that followed. *Halmeoni* had been in her box for about three days when I came inside from playing late one afternoon and saw, to my great surprise, my parents and *Unni* in the kitchen.

Look at that! I said to myself, astonished by this most unusual sight. How did they get a travel permit? I thought you could only get one when there was a death in the family …

A death in the family …

It was all starting to make sense. *Halmeoni*'s motionless body. All these people crying. My parents with their sudden travel permit. I remember the moment quite clearly. It was one of those times you never forget because of its peculiarity. I wasn't hurt anywhere, so I had no reason to feel ill, but just as water is used to prime a pump, so the events of the past few days had paved the way for a feeling that was to pursue me for a very long time: fear. I was afraid, without even knowing of what. I wished I were the black paste or the yellow liquid in the coffin so I could stay with *Halmeoni* in that box forever.

No one had told me about my parents' visit, and I was overwhelmed with happiness when I saw them. I ran to my father and grabbed his hand. He rarely held my hand but that day his handshake was so strong and loving that I forgot all the sorrow I'd felt upon seeing the sad expression on *Halmeoni*'s face.

I vaguely remember walking with the funeral procession which took the coffin to the mountain outside the village where our ancestors were buried. Finally, I understood that I would never see my beloved *Halmeoni* again. I watched as she disappeared once and for all under the white sheet that was placed over her before the coffin was sealed.

No more eggs for breakfast. No more stories about the moon and the sun. No more dancing chickens and foxes. Yet *Halmeoni* would live on forever deep inside me. I would never forget her, never replace her. It was as though, with this blank page placed over the past, she wanted to help me begin a new chapter of my life in the city and to give me a future full of light.

CHAPTER TWO

Halmeoni's death hastened my return to Ranam. My father brought everyone back from the country and was caring not only for my mother, *Unni* and me, but also for *Keun Abeoji*, my 'Great' Uncle, and *Jaguen Abeoji*, my 'Little' Uncle. Only Aunt *Gomo* stayed in the country.

'Great' Uncle had come down with the measles when he was a child, and he had had such a high fever that it affected his growth. His skin was damaged and he stuttered. He never set foot in school. Yet even though he was the laughing stock of the entire village, at home our family showed him the utmost respect. That is how *Halmeoni* had wanted it. She always had a soft spot for him, given his poor health, but she had also been particularly tough with him, because she didn't want his physical handicap to keep him from living his life. As the Korean saying goes, 'The greater your love for your child, the greater the need for the switch.'

With both parents gone, Great Uncle should have become the head of the family, but his mental and physical handicap prevented him from doing that. That responsibility therefore fell to my father, the second son.

'In Ranam, our future is full of hope,' he told us.

My father's sense of family, his energy and his optimism enriched our everyday lives, and despite our close quarters, Great Uncle and Little Uncle were both welcomed into our apartment. *How generous*, I think now, *especially on my mother's part*. She never complained about having two extra mouths to feed every day. It was customary to live with one or two of the husband's family members – a

Confucian tradition, in fact – but the four of us had already been living with so little.

My other uncle, *Il-rok*, whom I had never met, was in the army. Aunt *Gomo* stayed in the countryside to take care of the farm. She had never really been accepted by the family because she had a boyfriend but wasn't married to him. Everyone in the village was always pointing fingers at her, treating her as though she were the mistress of a married man. *Halmeoni*, too, made disparaging remarks, but *Gomo* always discreetly ignored them.

***

Now that we were in Ranam, it was time for me to start school. Living in the country, how I had dreamed of the day when I would return to the city, just as my sister had done. *Halmeoni* had already taught me to write, and I knew how to count without using my fingers. She had told me I had a good memory and would be a very good student.

On the first day of kindergarten, my parents took me to the *Moim Jangso*, the gathering point in front of the building where the military families lived and where our teacher came to fetch us. On the second day, I walked there by myself. My sister *Unni* had already started primary school and met up with her friends in a different place. Luckily, it was safe to walk alone in the road, which was unpaved and had no pavements, because there were no cars or trucks: owning a car was illegal in North Korea. Except for officers working for the Party, most people went everywhere on foot.

Han Hye-rim was my best friend. She often waited at the gathering point with me.

'*Annyong*, Hye-rim! (Hello!)' I cried. 'Jihyun!' She ran over to give me a hug.

'*Gonggui nori haja* (Let's play jacks),' I said. '*Soombak coqjil?* (How about hide-and-seek?)'

'*Hmmm … Julneomki haja gueureom* (We'll just have to play skipping rope),' I said.

'*Gueureoja* (OK),' Hye-rim agreed. Those moments were pure delight. We'd arrive early on purpose, and before the other kids from the neighbourhood arrived – forty or so boys and girls whose parents worked in the same factory as my father – Hye-rim and I would play and play until we were out of breath. She lived on the second floor of our building, in Flat No. 2. Her dad was the driver of the *Do Bowibu Jang*, the director of the National Security Detention Centre. Her mum was an *ajumma* like mine. Tall and slender, Hye-rim was the best dancer in our school. Delegations from Pyongyang would sometimes come to watch her dance, and she was always selected to take part in the big national events, such as Kim Il-sung's birthday or the New Year's Day celebration.

I'd known most of the children in the neighbourhood for a long time – since before I'd left for my grandmother's three years earlier. Some I knew less well than others but I was at ease with everyone. I loved my gang, we were all so full of life!

When I played, I tried not to get too dirty because I had only one set of clothes and I didn't want to make more work for *Eomeoni*, my mum. *Unni* had handed down her black polyester trousers to me, which she'd worn when she was my age, as well as a plain white T-shirt and a pair of *Pyeonliwha*, casual dark-blue canvas shoes. It wasn't really a uniform but it might as well have been, since everyone was dressed the same. There wasn't a very wide selection in the clothing section of Nam Chongjin's department store.

In the winter, I also wore a sweater that *Eomeoni* had knitted for me, and *Dongwha*, winter shoes, which came up to my ankles. I hated those shoes, because when it rained they got soaked and weighed a ton. I'll never forget all those pairs of shoes that my mother set beside the wood stove to dry on a rainy or snowy day – shoes everywhere!

On weekends, *Eomeoni* did the washing at the river five minutes from where we lived. She mostly went alone but always ran into *ajumma* from the neighbourhood there, and they would chat. In winter, she did the washing in the apartment because it was too cold to do it outside. She used a homemade soap made from the heads of *Jeongeori*, sardines – ideal for soap-making because they were both high in fat and low in cost. To make the soap, she would heat water in a big pot and throw in a handful of sardine heads. Once the water reached boiling point, she would add a product that helped the mixture solidify. She'd pour that into a wooden drawer she'd removed from a chest. Once the soap was set, she would cut it into small bars. The soap worked well on skin, hair, clothing ... except that it stank of fish!

Our teacher's name was Miss Kim, but we never called her by name, only *Sunsaengnim*, Teacher. She was petite, and her black suit became her. It made her look very strict, but I wasn't afraid of her at all. On the contrary, I found her quite nice. I was very fond of her. Every morning when she came to collect us at the *Moim Jangso*, she would divide us into four rows of ten.

'*Sohn jabgo!* (Hold hands!)' she'd say.

She'd stand at the head of the procession and lead us to school with a lively step while we sang our favourite hymn by Kim Il-sung – '*Pi Bada* (Sea of Blood)'. The hymn was part of the *Hyukmyeong Gagueuk*, a set of revolutionary operas that sang of the battle against the Japanese:

Let us join forces!
Let's go, let's go, let's go fight!
Let us be brave and fight with courage, no wavering!
These imperialist puppets are hastening their own demise
By committing ceaseless massacres and acts of barbarism.

We were the exalted heroes of the glorious fight, and we screamed the song the whole way to school until blue in the face.

School began at 8am. Mornings were devoted to maths, Korean and the life of Kim Il-sung. In the afternoon, we studied music or drawing. I found Korean a bit complicated. You had to take the *Gaguiapyo*, Korean alphabet chart, and copy it in its entirety, juxtaposing all ten vowels (A, YA, OE, YEO, O, YO, OU, YOO, EU and YI) with the fourteen consonants (G, N, D, R, M, B, S, silent H, J, TCH, K, T, P, H) to make syllables.

You started with G: G-A, G-YA, G-EO, G-YEO, G-O, G-YO, G-OU, G-YOO, G-EU, G-YI.

Next came N: N-A, N-YA, N-EO, N-YEO, N-O, N-YO, N-OU, N-YOO, N-EU, N-YI.

And so on, down to H, the final consonant.

I knew it was important to master the alphabet and I worked hard at it, but it was so boring! Today, my children in Manchester don't learn to read and write through simple-minded repetition. By contrast, I loved maths. I was always the first to finish writing out my numbers from 1 to 100. What counted was speed. *Halmeoni* was right: I was really good in school.

In the afternoon, while we learned songs about the life of Kim Il-sung in music class, *Sunsaengnim* played the accordion. How I looked up to my teacher! Not many people had the luxury of playing a musical instrument, especially not ordinary pupils like us. You had to be very special to attract the attention of the entourage, but once you were noticed you were sent to a school for gifted students, like my friend Hye-rim and her dance school. She would surely join the personal staff of *Sooryeongnim* Kim Il-sung, Our Leader, in Pyongyang – the supreme honour.

***

As I said, *Halmeoni* had been right when she told me having a good memory would serve me well, because we always learned everything by heart, starting with the birthdate of Kim Il-sung: 15 April 1912. *Sunsaengnim* had a distinct way of indicating his photograph, which hung on the wall: standing to the left of it, our teacher would raise her two hands together, palms facing up, bend her arms so her hands were shoulder height, then glide them towards the image. Even now, when you speak of The Portrait, you can't just say 'this picture'. You have to say, 'This picture to the left is that of our Beloved Father, Kim Il-sung.' You must never point at it – if you do, it's straight to the firing squad.

'There is one person who is more important than your own father,' said Teacher every day, 'and that is our dear General Kim Il-sung.'

Of course he was the most important person in the world; of course we must love him. His portrait was everywhere – on the red badges on our parents' jackets, on the wall in *Halmeoni*'s house (*Keun Aboeji,* my uncle, was responsible for cleaning it, because *Halmeoni* was too short to reach it), on the streets, in the trains, in the railway stations, in the newspapers. There was also a giant statue of him in the park, at the foot of which we placed flowers on his birthday.

My father also told us that we must address our New Year's wishes to our Beloved Father before addressing them to our parents:

Kyungae haneun Aboeji,
Dearly Beloved Father,
Kim Il-sung wonsunim,
His Excellency Kim Il-sung,
Gomapseumnida,
I thank you.

The class 'The Life of Kim Il-sung' quickly became my favourite. A daily lesson that lasted forty minutes, it took place in a room called *Kim Il-sung Hyukmyeong Yeoksa Yeongusil,* History of the Korean Revolution under Kim Il-sung Research Room. Located next to the Headmaster's office, the room was kept carefully locked with a key only the Headmaster carried. To enter that sacred chamber, whose four white walls were completely covered in photographs of Kim Il-sung, we'd follow our teacher single file, placing our index finger on our lips – *Shhh!* – because we mustn't speak a word. We donned our white cloth slippers, *Beoseon,* that just covered our feet, stopping below the ankle. Our mothers sewed them especially for this purpose, because ordinary socks were forbidden lest they leave marks.

The first time I entered this heavenly room I was so nervous, I could hear my own heart beating in the silence. The first photo I saw was of Kim Il-sung in 1926. He was a schoolboy, wearing a black uniform with metal buttons and a matching black cap. *Sunsaengnim* explained to us that we were to memorise everything that was written under each photograph. And there were forty photographs in all! She and our parents would help us, she said, since we still didn't know how to read very well. But I loved this class – I dreamed of coming back to that enchanted place, that sanctuary.

The photograph that made the deepest impression on me showed the house with the thatched roof in which our General had grown up. I'd spent most of my life in an apartment and had never seen a house like this one. My grandmother had lived in a house, of course, but it was an ordinary one, not so old, with a tiled roof and white walls. I was intrigued by the three pots in the photo: they were sitting outside the house. One was broken and lying on its side. *Our Beloved Father must have been truly poor*, I said to myself, for I had never seen the likes, even at home. *Eomeoni* would never use a broken pot.

Sunsaengnim explained that Kim Il-sung had been born into poverty in a district called *Mankyungdae* in Pyongyang. Though he started with nothing, he rose to become a world leader of the twentieth century, waging war and working his entire life to bring happiness to the people of North Korea.

This was a revelation! So, it was thanks to *him* that we were alive, that we had food to eat and a roof over our heads. It was then that I understood why we took such good care of his portrait at home and at *Halmeoni*'s, and why we called him 'Commander with the Iron Will' *Kangchul eui Yeongoung*, 'Unique Star' *Han Byeol*, 'Our General' *Janggoon-nim*, 'Our Commander in Chief' *Wonsu-nim* and 'Our Leader' *Sooryeong-nim*.

We owed him everything. My friends and I longed for only one thing: to stand together before Him and be amazed.

That evening, *Abeoji* caught me staring at the portrait that hung on the wall across from the cupboard. I'd been standing and staring even longer than usual.

'*Abeoji*, why must we love Kim Il-sung, *Sooryeongnim*, Revered Leader, more than you? Aren't you our real father?' I asked, as though I wanted confirmation of all that had been revealed to me in school that day to come from his own lips.

'Shhh, don't say that, the neighbours can hear you!' he warned. 'I know this might seem strange to you now, but you'll understand when you're a little older. We must respect *Sooryeongnim* and be loyal to him. It's thanks to him that we know what happiness is. For the time being, you must do as you're told at school and work hard. That's the only way to honour him, understand?'

'*Neh, Abeoji* (Yes, Papa),' I murmured.

I was only too happy to believe him. We never spoke of it again.

***

Ever since coming back to Ranam I had been hungry. Mom displayed feats of imagination in order to put food in our bowls every day, but it wasn't enough. Unlike *Halmeoni*, she never gave me eggs or apples. My stomach growled constantly, especially at night. I would curl up on the floor to make myself forget, but hunger often kept me from sleeping. The next day, it was same thing all over again. I was only six years old but never complained – I knew it would do no good.

At least at nursery we were given a hot meal every day: one bowl of rice and one bowl of soup. Before eating, we would all say, '*Abeoji gomabseubnida* (Thank you, Beloved Father).' After all, it was He who gave us our meals.

We knew it was time for lunch when we smelled *Doenjang*, fermented soybean paste. The team in charge of serving lunch – three of us, myself included – would hurtle down the stairs towards the kitchen, which was located in the basement. The rice would be cooking in a pot over a wood fire. My pals took care of the soup while I carried back up the stairs a big metal tray crammed with bowls of rice. After placing it on my head, I held it steady with both hands – I was one of the stronger, more nimble kids and therefore thrilled to have been chosen for such a delicate operation. We ate our meal in silence. The whole ritual lasted barely ten minutes. After all, a bowl of rice and a bowl of soup don't take long to eat. As soon as we finished, we took the bowls back downstairs: our lunch break was over.

After lunch, *Sunsaegnim* would have us lie down on the floor for a nap, but I never managed to sleep. I could hardly wait for the hour to be up so that we could do our wake-up calisthenics. We would move to the rhythm of the *Inmin bogueon chejo*, calisthenics for the health of the people, following *Sunsaengnim*'s commands:

'*Pahl beolligo* (Open your arms wide) …'
'*Soom shuigo* (Take a deep breath) …'
'*Pahl jeobgo* (Close your arms) …'
'*Soom shuigo* (Take a deep breath) …'

Hana, dul, set, net … One, two three, four … To this staccato rhythm we performed each movement. Precision was everything. Chants of solidarity and common effort, encouraging words from our comrades: this was the world of my childhood, and in this world we felt indispensable.

Our days were scheduled right down to the minute. During the only other break besides lunch, we had barely enough time to go to the bathroom. Classes ended at 5pm, after which the teacher returned us to the gathering point. From there, everyone returned home. Sometimes we were handed a few biscuits or *Peong-peong-yi*, puffed corn, but most of the time we were starving so we ran to that other source of food: home.

Every time I entered our building, I was struck by the slightly sweet scent of corn cooking. Everyone started cooking at the same time, and the aroma filled the corridors.

Sometimes you could smell chestnuts roasting. That reminded me of *Halmeoni*. We missed her; we missed the chickens and the snakes and the foxes, too. Such wonderful memories! During the curfew periods, which would plunge Ranam into darkness for an hour or two each evening, my uncles, sister and I would huddle together and recall our happy times spent in the countryside.

***

Hanging from the wall opposite the glass-enclosed booth in our building's entryway was a brass bell. At 5am every morning, the *Inminbanjang*, group leader, would take a metal hammer and vigorously strike the bell. As the person in charge of the life of the building, that was her first job of the day. One bell would ring, then two, then three ... What sounded at first like an echo was actually the consecutive ringing of the other bells in the neighbourhood: one in the building opposite, one in the building behind us, and the bells of the three other buildings. It was a chaotic concerto, vibrations resonating and reverberating from building to building, spreading like a contagion. This was a rare moment, when you could actually revel in a sense of mayhem – something otherwise unimaginable in a society so structured.

'*Cheongso haro na-o-seyo*! (Everyone come out, time to clean!)' yelled the group leader.

Each apartment was assigned specific tasks: No. 2 cleaned the floors. No. 6, the windows. No. 5 was charged with dusting. The tasks rotated every week. If you missed the bell and were late, the group leader would come knocking on your door.

'*Na-o-seyo!* (Come out!)' she'd yell. Once the building had been cleaned, the group leader had to organise the weekly meeting. The person in whose apartment the meeting was held would read aloud a hand-out which had been written for the group by Kim Il-sung. Most often it was a speech or some piece of news or information sent to the group leader from City Hall. That is how housewives like my mother were kept abreast of our Leader's thinking. The meetings were also opportunities to hold self-criticism sessions, *Saenghwal Cheongwha*. If you had failed to do your duty, you had to own up to it. For example, 'Yesterday I didn't clean the corridor' or 'I forgot to dust The Portrait'. Each confession was meticulously recorded in the register by the group leader.

Eomeoni often came home tired from these meetings because there wasn't a single moment of rest during the day. She explained, though, that if we didn't have a rigorous system in place people would become lazy and dishonest, and in a revolutionary socialist state like ours such a thing was unthinkable.

Like all the other *ajumma* in the building, my mum prepared breakfast at 5am every morning. *Unni*, the eldest child, did the cleaning in her place. Sometimes my father did it, but only rarely. In theory, women were men's equals, but in practice that's not exactly how it played out. I might have been taller, but *Unni* was the oldest: she did chores on the building while I helped inside the apartment.

Every day when I came home from school, my mother would ask me to do my homework before going out to play. I had to write out the Korean alphabet five times and my numbers from one to one hundred five or six times too. Then, staring at the clock that hung on the wall next to the portrait of Kim Il-sung, I had to practise telling time.

Lighting a candle to save electricity, *Unni* and I would sit at the wooden folding table –the same one on which our meals were served – and do our homework together. Homework offered us our very own kingdom, our refuge. In spite of the years we had lived apart from each other, my sister and I were very close.

'How can you not know that, huh?' *Unni* would tease me, a smile playing at the corner of her lips.

We bought plain wooden pencils and paper at the Nam Chongjin department store. The pencils were very expensive; we only got one each. My mother would cut them into two pieces, setting aside one half in case we lost the other one. Then she'd sharpen the pencils with a knife.

Once I had finished my homework, I could go outside and play. It rarely happened, but how I loved to run into my father on his way home from work, driving his red tractor. I was so proud of him – not only because he was a model citizen who believed in the regime, but especially because he drove a red Russian-made forklift truck!

He'd park across from our building and all my friends would run to gather round it once *Abeoji* had stepped down. I never missed a chance to brag:

'This is the only red forklift truck in Chongjin!'

'Really?'

'Yeah! There are only three in the whole country, and this is one of them!'

'You are so lucky! Can we climb on it? Come on, please?'

'No way! It's not for little brats like you, keep off!'

I'd sit up on the tractor seat, indifferent to their banter. He was *my* father and this was *our* red tractor.

Despite my arrogant displays, I had a lot of friends. 'How can you be so different from your sister? She's such a good girl, so quiet and respectful, while you're always roaming about like a tomboy!' my grandmother used to say when we lived in the countryside. It's true, I was always out chasing snakes and foxes. And I did get into lots of fights. One day I came upon a friend of mine making fun of my mother:

'… the fat mama of the neighbourhood,' she said.

'What did you say? Maybe she is fat, what's it to you? At least we're rich, *Yi gannashiki*, you little bitch!'

'*Jeo gannashiki*, you're the bitch! Take that!'

And then came the hair-pulling and the biting.

I didn't know why my mother was so overweight. I had only ever known her like that. The day I was born, my father had been sent to work in Musan, a city on the border with China. Mum had to give birth at home, all alone. After the birth her health worsened, but for all their free care the hospitals were no help at all – there simply wasn't a single competent doctor around, and no adequate medicine or medical equipment. A month and a half later, my father, desperate, was finally granted special permission to return to Chongjin on leave and meet his newborn child. He brought my mother *Sancheong*, which he believed to be a rare type of honey. It was a luxury food, and although it did help her get well, the sugary stuff made her retain water and she gained a lot of weight. People simply thought she was fat because she was rich.

It's a subject that would wreak havoc more than once between me and my friends. But even more absorbing was my favourite pastime, playing war:

'Those American dogs are teaming up with the dirty South Koreans to destroy our rich and powerful country! Who wants to be the good guys?'

'I do! I wanna be a North Korean soldier!'

'No, I wanna be that!'

'Me too!'

'Not fair! I always have to play a South Korean bastard!'

'And I always have to be with the treacherous Americans!'

'Enemy of the people! Die, you southern trash!'

'Ouch! Eee! Argh!'

We ran around hitting each other with sticks. It was utter chaos and buckets of fun.

'Long live the Fatherland! *Grrrrrr*! I am a child of victorious Korea! I give my life to build our Great Democratic Republic!'

Swept up by my friends' cries, I was a noble, proud and patriotic child, happy to live under Kim Il-sung's protection. In South Korea, the children were so poor they couldn't even go to school and many of them died of hunger. Thanks to our dear General, we were descended from an intelligent people, heroes of the great war of liberation from the Japanese.

My friend Hye-rim was part of our gang. Her mother didn't like having people in their apartment, so we'd call up to her from the street to see if she could come out to play. She had two little sisters, and was lucky enough to live with her grandmother and aunt as well. Unlike me, she didn't have to help her mother with the domestic chores so she could play a lot longer than I could, but sometimes we'd stay out until 10pm.

Hye-rim and I loved to look up at the starry sky. We'd take deep, quiet breaths. In school, we had learned a little astrology, and together we'd search the skies for the Plough. There were stars everywhere. So many that even I, who was so good at maths, couldn't count them all. The sky was abundant, beautiful, peaceful; the twinkling stars overwhelmed us. If I were to go back to Ranam one day, I'm not certain the stars would shine so brightly.

As for *Unni*, she never left the house. We always did our homework with each other, but we never played together. A model eldest daughter, she didn't have a lot of friends and spent her time reading books about the Kim family. All our neighbours paid her compliments for being so exemplary. I was proud of her!

On 15 April, our class celebrated the birthday of Kim Il-sung. We all went to the park in Ranam to see the bronze statue of him as a student, wearing a cap and holding a book under his arm. The statue must have been 3–4 metres tall but to me it was as high as a hill, the very hill we climbed to gather flowers to place at its feet.

So many people cleaned and polished the statue that it gleamed like the stairwell in our building. We kids were responsible for sweeping the ground around it. Our teacher asked us to bring our own brooms – short-handled ones, made of rice husks – as well as our own dustpans. She'd give the signal, and forty little brooms would begin their frenetic sweeping. We'd scurry around like busy ants until the place was impeccably clean.

That date was also the day *Unni* and I rose before sunrise in anticipation of the rice cakes to come. *Eomeoni* always prepared *Songpyeon*, cakes made of white rice with red bean paste inside; *Jeolpyeon*, square rice cakes with nothing inside; and *Chalddeokk*, cakes made from ground rice. The portions on 15 April were generous. As a rule, I was the one who went to the rationing centre to bring back the supplies. After waiting in line for many long hours I would bring back two eggs, oil, bean sprouts, tofu, pork, 1 kilogram of rice flour and 100 grams of sweets per person.

Even with these special rations, *Eomeoni* would have to save her rice for months and months ahead of time in order to have enough rice flour to make seven *Songpyeon* per family member. We never fought over our cakes, but my mother always counted them out, out of a sense of fairness – it was such a rare and special occasion, she didn't want anyone to go short. There were three national holidays – the birthday of Kim Il-sung, the anniversary of the founding of the Party, and New Year's Day – and these were the only times in the year when we got to taste those rice cakes. Sweet as honey, they melted in our mouths.

I adored my sister, but if I touched her things without her permission she'd go red with anger. She even kept her rice cakes hidden, saving them for later so she could savour them at her leisure. I on the other hand ate all of mine straight away. Today, I still do that, never saving anything for later. Sometimes my sister would hide her treats so well she couldn't remember where she'd left them and would ask me to help her search. I helped her willingly, but found her a bit dumb in those cases!

Everyone pampered *Unni* because she was the eldest girl. Of course I was jealous, but I couldn't hold it against her, nor could I complain: *Abeoji* had drilled it into me that I must never get into a fight with her, for she was my older sister and I must show her respect. I also had to show my parents absolute obedience. If I were to name one thing North Koreans do well, it's instilling respect for elders.

My sister loved noodle soup. She was happy that *Eomeoni* prepared it so often. It was made with fermented soybeans, to which our mother added corn noodles. She boiled the noodles a long time so they would plump up, filling the bowl. Personally, I thought it was vile. I never liked that dish. I knew, though, that *Eomeoni* struggled to find enough food with which to feed the whole family, so I ate without complaint. Mom often sent me to the neighbours to collect noodles in return for the ones she had given them as an advance. She always sent me, never my sister – she knew I had a certain character and would not come home empty-handed. I had no idea then how destitute the people were from whom I took those noodles – I was only doing my job.

Unni was allowed not to like the smell of fish. She was allowed to leave pork fat on her plate. *She* was allowed, *I* was not. I made myself eat everything without being picky, but she didn't even try. I couldn't understand why my parents put up with it – to me it was unfair but I didn't say anything. Especially not to my sister – never a bad word nor an inappropriate gesture.

One day while we were playing the in the apartment, I jostled my younger uncle, *Jaguen Abeoji*. More of an older brother than an uncle to me, he was only fourteen when I met him for the first time at *Halmeoni*'s house and it was he who initiated me when it came to life in the country. He had shown me how to catch dragonflies and eat frog's legs. Since then, we had stayed best friends and we played together all the time.

That day, without meaning to, I scratched his arm slightly. He wasn't hurt – he laughed it off – but my mother flew into a rage, accusing me of wounding my uncle and disrespecting him. Her words seemed unjustified to me, but as usual, not a word passed my lips.

To shake off the intense feeling of unfairness, I locked myself in the toilet and cried for a long time. That helped me blow off steam. I splashed cold water on my face and felt better. Washed clean of my sorrow, I emerged as though nothing had happened.

CHAPTER THREE

It's hard to know what's on other people's minds. I liked school because I loved to learn, and I thought the rest of the class was like me. But I'm not so sure any more. It's possible that some of my classmates were experts at pretending and hid behind their smiles ....

September 1974: that's when I started primary school in Bongnam. I was seven years old. Located a half-hour's walk from home, the school had been built during Japanese rule. The exterior walls were yellowish beige, rather than the faded red brick of the other buildings in Ranam which I was accustomed to, and inside the floors were made of wood. I mention this because there was a whole ritual about the floors, which had to be cleaned every day, and that was a chore that ended up claiming a lot of my time. You had to push all the desks to the back of the classroom and clean the floor in the front – first with a wet mop, then with dry cloths. After that, you had to apply wax. Then you had to push all the desks to the front and wash the floor at the back of the classroom. Finally, when you finished cleaning, you had to put all the desks back in their places. Luckily, I would become class delegate within a few months, which spared me from such insufferable tasks. To my huge relief, I could oversee the cleaning instead of doing it myself.

There were about fifty girls in my class, all from the same kindergarten; there were boys in the school, too, but in a separate classroom. I can still see all those tiny desks, each with barely enough room for two pencils and two workbooks. I shared my desk with Gum-ok Lee – she wasn't a very good student and I didn't like her much. Her nose ran constantly, which earned her the nickname *Kho Heulligae*, 'Snotty Nose'. The fact that her trousers were too short and had holes in the knees didn't help. Our teacher often asked me to help her with her homework. I forced myself because I didn't want to disobey *Sunsaengnim*, but I couldn't stand wasting my time on her – I had trouble enough getting my own work done.

Bok-soon was in my class, too. She was my second-best friend, after Hye-rim. An accomplished accordionist, she had been taught by her mother. With her perfectly fair complexion and bow-shaped lips, she was extremely beautiful and very cultured. She even took books to read in the toilet! On the other hand, she was a year older than the rest of us because her mother had enrolled her late in school, and Bok-soon paid the price:

'Hey, *Moogueun Doeji!* (Old Pig!),' I shouted. 'What? Cut it out!'

'Cut *what* out? You're an old pig! Not my fault if you're older than we are!' I laughed.

Bok-soon would pretend to be angry, but deep down I knew she didn't care – she knew full well it was just a big joke between us.

At the end of primary school, I lost touch with Gum-ok 'Snotty Nose' Lee. *Does she still live in the flats in Ranam where we grew up?* I often wonder what became of my childhood friends. When people talk about seeing their friends from school again, I'm envious. Such a seemingly simple thing, but for me, it's impossible.

***

To my eyes, our teacher, Kim Gun-gok, was the most beautiful woman in the world. She was young, having just finished her studies at university. Like Bok-soon, she had a perfectly round face and porcelain skin. With her smile and her long ebony hair, she looked like a poet's muse. She exuded happiness and contentment – until the day she got married and came back to school with her hair cut short and permed, *ajumma*-style. Her new husband couldn't stand her straight hair, which made her look girlish. I think she wasn't very happy in her marriage.

Fifty girls in five rows of ten would sit at their desks, staring at her. Each held a book – or rather, a photocopy of a book made by our mothers at the request of *Sunsaengnim*, because there were never enough – in her hands, arms outstretched, eyes on the blackboard, eager to quench her thirst for knowledge. Working hard in school is all we knew how to do, and it's all our parents and teachers expected from us. 'Hard work is how we show our loyalty to our beloved Father Kim Il-sung!' Those words hammered my ears day and night, during every lesson, every minute, in school, at home, and we always answered them with '*Neh!*' – an energetic if rote 'yes' – without raising an eyebrow.

Every morning, our teacher would ask us to clean the portrait of Kim Il-sung with the white cloth that sat on her desk. More than ten times a month this honour fell to me. As much as I despised washing the floor at the end of the day, how I loved dusting The Portrait! It was a chore that was only assigned to the very best students, and I was thrilled to be among them. Every time I did it, I seized the occasion to memorise the excerpts from Kim Il-sung's speeches, which hung on either side of the photograph.

Our school uniform consisted of a white T-shirt and black trousers. I took good care of mine because the trousers were made of wool and my mother had paid dearly for them – 50 won! – at the department store in Nam Chongjin. My father, I knew, only earned 120 won a month. You could tell who was rich by the length of their trouser legs: those who could afford it had new trousers as they grew taller, those who couldn't wore trousers that were too short for them.

Every week at school there were two important meetings which no one could afford to miss. The first was the General Assembly, which lasted about forty-five minutes and took place on Saturday afternoons, and the second was the Meeting on Daily Life. The names were different, but they were in effect occasions for students to do self-criticism. Everybody had a field day, denouncing anyone who arrived late or made noise or showed disrespect:

'She scribbled in her workbook during the history lesson on Kim Il-sung!' one pupil would declare.

'Do you know that being distracted is a very serious insult to the Leader of our Nation? Let us hear your self-criticism,' the teacher would say to the accused pupil.

'During history class, I was distracted and I scribbled on my workbook,' the accused pupil would answer. 'I did not know the consequences of my actions. I will never do it again. I will make up for it by working very hard to serve our fatherland and become a servant who is worthy of our socialist state. Please forgive me.'

'You must write out your self-criticism ten times by tomorrow. Do you understand?'

'Yes, Teacher.'

I often got up at four in the morning to review my homework, but I also did it so I wouldn't be criticised – even though it was almost impossible to avoid that! I, too, had to criticise my pals: I had to say who had got a bad grade, had to denounce those who had behaved badly. Everyone without exception had to do it. Some children cried when they were criticised. My friends and I made deals, agreeing on what each of us would critique in the other. For example, I made a deal with Hye-rim and Bok-soon that they would criticise me and I would criticise them. If by chance someone else came along and criticised one of us, it made me furious! The teachers, too, had their own meetings in the Headmaster's office, during which they did their own obligatory self-criticism. I remember the time when, after I'd become a maths teacher myself, a colleague of mine was criticised: she was pregnant, and the nausea had for a short time prevented her from doing her job well.

At least there was no chance of me scribbling during the history lesson – it was my favourite class! We learned that Kim Il-sung had completely rebuilt the country which the Korean War of 1953 had destroyed. When he was barely fourteen, he set out alone for China to get an education. He walked more than 1,600 kilometres. Every 14 January, we would walk 130 kilometres out of solidarity and to commemorate his journey. *At fourteen I'll do the same thing*, I told myself. *I'll help rebuild my country. But I won't leave, for we have everything we need, there is no reason to envy the rest of the world*, as we sang on that occasion:

No Reason to Envy the Rest of the World
The sky is blue
My heart is so light
The sound of the accordion floats through the air
People live together in harmony
I love my homeland
Our beloved father Kim Il-sung
Our home, the embrace of the Party
We are all brothers and sisters
With nothing to envy in the whole world.

'*People live together in harmony* ...' As a child I believed I was happy, but I don't know if I was happy because I was told I was, or if I truly was. My happiness was prescribed, and it came with operating instructions: solidarity, collective life, optimism. The dosage? Take some every hour for twelve hours a day and every hour for twelve hours a night.

It's true, our days were so full they didn't leave time for thinking or mulling over one's fate. Every hour, every minute, we had to learn something. Even as we slept we couldn't wait to rise the next morning and rush back to work. Was it this inability to think that allowed us to be, in a certain way, happy?

Missing school was unheard of. When the teacher called the register, no one was ever absent. I went to school even when I was sick. When on occasion someone *was* missing, Teacher first sent the class representative to the home of the student in question and then, if it was serious –if the child was dying of hunger, for example – she would go herself. I hadn't had childhood diseases like chicken pox or measles, but some of my friends had. They'd had to stay home in a sort of quarantine. 'One Hundred Days of Sun' – *baik il hae*, or whooping cough – was a sickness that caused a fever lasting for months and months. Luckily, no one in my family caught it: one could not afford to be weak for the Kim family. At school we were vaccinated against polio, tuberculosis and measles, and once a year we were given deworming medication – that was about it when it came to medical care.

***

Our little family was growing. On 8 January 1976, when my mother was thirty-one, she gave birth to her third child. It was a freezing cold night. Through the window I could see the snow that had accumulated in the streets of Chongjin. *Eomeoni* always came home exhausted after her long days of work, but that evening she seemed more tired than usual and complained of pain in her belly. My father had come home early that day and immediately took control of the situation, sending us to spend the night at the neighbours'. I liked the neighbours well enough and this was a break from our daily routine, so I was happy for this unexpected change. It was only returning home the next morning that I realised the baby was on its way. The women in the building had taken over from *Abeoji*, who had had to return to the factory. He could not miss a day of work just because his wife was about to give birth. Such a thing was unthinkable.

My sister and I had taken refuge in the kitchen, where the wood stove kept us warm. The old midwife – really just an *ajumma* like any other, but one who helped women give birth at no charge – was also there. We tried to follow what was happening by looking through the little window into the main room, but in vain. Suddenly we heard the midwife cry, 'You have a little brother!' We heard the baby let out a wail and ran into the room to see him. Following the midwife's orders, *Unni* went to boil water in the kitchen. When she came back, she took the baby in her arms and held him to her. As for me, I wasn't very useful and felt a bit bored, so I went outside to play. When my father came home that night, he got very emotional – he was proud to have a baby boy at last. He named him Jeong-ho and went off to the police station that very day to register the birth.

I was very happy to have a baby brother, but something was bothering me: from now on, I would have to settle for being third. My sister, the eldest, would always hold the highest place in everyone's mind. Next came my brother, because he was a boy. And I came in third place. I didn't like coming in last, it didn't suit me at all.

Later that year, after Jeong-ho's birth, to celebrate the New Year, relatives from my mother's side of the family came to visit from Chongjin. My aunt gave my sister and brother more pocket money than she gave me – they each got 30 won, whereas I only got 20. In a fit of rage, I slammed the door to the toilet, where I often retreated when I was unhappy. I told myself that the pocket money would end up with my mother anyway and she would use it to buy uniforms and pencils and workbooks. And yet the principle of equality – the very bedrock of my upbringing – had not been respected, and that hurt. Without knowing it, I had become a child for whom principles mattered.

My mother allowed herself one day to recover from my brother's birth. The next day, she was already up and about, taking care of our apartment and the building as usual. According to both North and South Korean tradition, a mother should rest 100 days after giving birth, but since *Eomeoni* had neither a mother nor a sister of her own to help her, and because she had to go right back to work, she wrapped her new baby in a *bojagui*, a square of fabric, and carried him on her back as she once again took up her duty washing the walls. The child was healthy, and she was able to breastfeed him, so she had nothing to complain about. *Unni* changed his nappies and gave him his bath. She washed the dirty nappies by hand. Between the stench of the nappies and the fishy-smelling soap, I stayed clear of the toilet!

Soon after my brother was born I became very independent. I did my homework by myself, I did the laundry (except for the nappies) by myself, and I cleaned the house myself. *Unni* cooked and washed the dishes and took care of me and Jeong-ho. She was the eldest girl and she was really good at it, calm and hardworking and meticulous. I, on the other hand, was gung-ho, full of energy and enthusiasm! We made a good team.

***

On 16 February 1978, Kim Jong-Il's birthday, I was invited to take an entrance exam to the *Sonyundan*, or Corps of Young Pioneers. Founded by Kim Il-sung on 6 June 1932, this was an organisation made up of seven-to-thirteen-year-olds. The purpose was to train revolutionary fighters under the orders of the Great Commander in Chief of the Communist Party. Learning five new songs and studying forty pages on the life of Kim Il-sung, in addition to taking care of my little brother with no help from anybody, was a lot of work, but I was so thrilled to think of wearing the Red Scarf around my neck that I threw myself into it. Not only did you need good grades in school – otherwise you couldn't even apply – but you also had to have the right *songbun*, that is, you had to come from the right class. This was a concept our maths teacher had taught us one day before class: '*Songbun* is a classification system the Workers Party established in 1957. It divides Korean citizenry into political, social, and economic groups, so you see, your fate depends entirely on this! Each of you, without exception, has an ancestral *songbun* that was established on 9 September 1948, the day our State was created, and which reflects what your family did that day.'

The entire class listened, silent, mouths agape, like so many dead mice crushed under the weight of those words.

'We distinguish three main categories,' the teacher went on, though in reality there are more than fifty. 'The superior class, called *Baekdu Hyultong*, is the line to which Kim Il-sung belongs. This is the "loyal" class, those who fought the Japanese during the war. Next is the middle or "neutral" class, the *Joonggan Cheung*, made up of ordinary people who haven't necessarily wronged the Party. And finally, there is the lower or "hostile" class, or *Jeokdae Cheung*, the people who have a family member who's defected to the South, or who have wronged the Party or committed dangerous crimes.'

I knew we belonged to the superior class, thanks to our paternal grandfather, who had fought the Japanese with Kim Hyeong-kwon, Kim Il-sung's uncle, in the 1930s. We had no idea what he looked like – there was not a single photograph of him at home. He was from Jeolla Province in the South, and while he had managed to join the upper class, he hadn't managed to become a well-known public figure. I also knew that my mother's *songbun* was not as good as my father's, but I didn't know why. Your father's *songbun* counted more than your mother's, anyway. The professor ended his comments with a rather chilling remark: 'Your *songbun* can change over the course of your lifetime. You can attain a higher class by serving your country with a heroic act, but you may also drop into a lower category if you commit an undesirable act, and your family will be affected for three generations to come! So if you don't want to be downgraded, you'd best behave!'

So it was thanks to my father's good standing that I qualified to take the *Sonyundan* entrance exam. The exam was offered only three times a year: on 16 February, Kim Jong-Il's birthday; on 15 April, Kim Il-sung's birthday; and on 6 June, when the Corps of Young Pioneers was formed. Only two other girls, Ok-seo and Ma Hyang-suk, had been invited to take the exam along with me. They too were at the top of their class, and their parents were Party members. The father of Ok-seo was an accountant who worked for the Bureau of Housing Construction, an important position. My friend Hye-rim was not invited, so she had to wait until 15 April. When I passed my exam brilliantly and was called to receive my red scarf, she was jealous.

The day was freezing cold, so the ceremony was held in a local cinema. The cinema consisted of a room with white walls, wooden chairs and a large projector at the back. Families were not invited, so I went with my friends from school. The Headmaster congratulated us and made a speech about the importance of wearing the red scarf. The teachers tied the scarves around our necks, and we then bowed and saluted with a hearty *Choongseong!* (At your service!) Once I got home, I kept the red scarf on all night.

***

In my opinion, the true political education in North Korea begins when you join the Corps of Young Pioneers. It started with extra hours after the normal school day. My sister, *Unni*, joined too. Why be loyal to Kim Il-sung? Which countries were our enemies? South Korea, Japan, the United States … 'Down with the Americans, destroyers of Korea!' was the refrain. It was their fault our country was divided and at war with itself! How I hated them. At home, my parents criticised the Americans a lot, too.

Until I joined the Corps of Young Pioneers, I had played with any friend, regardless of his or her social status, but since becoming a Pioneer I'd also gained an awareness that I was not to play with anyone from a lower *songbun* than mine. Which is why, one April day in 1984, I decided I would no longer play with Hwang Hye-ryeon. She was a good friend of mine, but because her father was not a member of the Party, I told myself, she must be bad. I was making a terrible mistake, and I realise that now, but at the time I felt no guilt whatsoever.

We were taught to hate. Hye-ryeon was from South Hwanghae Province. Her family was discredited because they were landowners when the State was formed. One day she asked me if she could play skipping, and I told her there were too many kids and I couldn't accept her into the group. I still miss her today – she was really funny and we'd got on very well. Therefore, I mostly played with Lee Hyang-suk, Hye-lim and Bok-soon. The professors treated all the pupils the same and didn't reveal anyone's *songbun*. We found these things out for ourselves at the beginning of the year, when we filled out the forms where we had to indicate our father's profession and say whether or not he was a Party member. Children were actually banished – they would have no more schooling for the rest of their lives – if their grandparents had been critical of Kim Il-sung in the past.

A society whose hierarchy is determined by social status but that sees itself as being 'the country of the socialist miracle'. When I think about it now, such deceit! Especially since having good *songbun* didn't necessarily mean having a better life. Your *songbun* did determine the range of opportunities that were open to you, and *Unni*, Jeong-ho and I, children from an ordinary family, neither rich nor poor, were about to experience that fact very soon.

This was around the time a very important episode in my life took place. In 1978, my mother began raising pigs. The government, needing to feed the army, required that all families raise pigs and offer them as gifts as a way of proving their devotion and gratitude.

Every flat in our building came with a small outdoor shed for storing coal, wood and pots of kimchi. To make room for the pigs, my mother dug out the floor of our shed. Pig husbandry was no easy undertaking and the lazier families proved rather untroubled by the new order, preferring to live on their rations without raising pigs. But my mother told us it was worth it, that we'd be able to eat pork more often and that it was important to contribute to feeding the army. We were among the first to embark on this adventure. Gradually other families set about doing it too and before long you couldn't walk around outside without hearing a pig grunting on every street corner. They were noisy, for sure, but they weren't dirty and they didn't stink – and that was a blessing!

Unni and I were responsible for feeding these pigs. We ran all over our block of flats collecting people's vegetable peelings and the water used to rinse their rice. With no lift, we had to run up three flights of stairs, stopping at every floor to knock on the door of all ten flats – and then do that again in a series of other buildings. It was really tiring; I hated doing it but I didn't have a choice. Little by little, our pigs multiplied. My mother would take our females to a neighbour who was raising a male and she would leave them there for a week. I smile when I think of her herding the pigs, hitting their rumps with a stick and me running along behind, yelping with laughter. Before too long we found ourselves with fifteen pigs. One or two were set aside each year for the government. The suckling pigs my mother sold when they were born. Getting wind of this, people would line up in front of our shed to buy them.

My mother was happy both to be successful with the pigs and to be contributing to the army's well-being. The first time she killed a pig – and she killed two per year – she served part of it to us for dinner, and we were even allowed a little white rice! Part of the meat was set aside to be smoked and the rest was sold. I was quite proud of my mother for setting up her little business, even if it caused her some trouble. The authorities had asked the people to raise pigs and then offer them up; they had not given people the right to sell them. Jealous of my mother's success, the neighbours really went after her during the weekly criticism sessions. Moreover, she'd developed a taste for the money the pigs brought in and over time kept raising her prices! Using the money she set aside, she was able to give us white rice and new clothes. This was the first time since leaving *Halmeoni*'s home that I had enough to eat.

No one suspected that this business would break our family into 1,000 pieces.

***

My little brother Jeong-ho was a very clever boy and a fast learner. At one, he was walking; at two, he was talking – his first word was his own name. Because my mother was busy with the pigs, and because Jeong-ho couldn't go to nursery school (our mother didn't officially work), I took care of him a lot. We played hide-and-seek and Kill the Americans. I also taught him to catch dragonflies, as my 'Little' Uncle had taught me, and to play house in the sand pile in front of our flat – I'd put sand in pieces of broken glass and pretend I was serving rice in bowls. When I did my homework, though, he was on his own: like me at his age, he had to learn to take care of himself and play alone.

In the summer of 1978, my uncle Il-rok completed his military service and paid us a surprise visit. He had a free week ahead of him, before starting his job in the Gueumdok mines in Dancheon, South Hamgyong Province, home to the biggest zinc mines in all of Southeast Asia. As a gift, he brought us a big bag of apricots. It was the first time I had ever seen one! We were so excited, almost delirious at the sight of these fruits we'd never before tasted. But despite all the commotion the fruit caused, my uncle had a quiet way about him and said little. He was fair-skinned, with a beautiful complexion and eyes like a girl's. I was happy he'd introduced me to apricots but I didn't find him very interesting – he wasn't funny like my two other uncles.

We were still admiring the apricots when Great Uncle Il-seop and Little Uncle Myeon-sik came home from Ryongam, where they had been working in the fields since six in the morning.

'*Hyungnim* (Big brother!),' cried Little Uncle Myeon-sik, running to greet him.

'*Myeong-sik*? (How are you?)'

'How long has it been since we've seen each other?'

Silence.

My father couldn't hold back his tears; he hadn't seen his brother for sixteen years and he was very emotional. He sat on the floor and, reaching behind him, pulled the low table on which we ate our meals towards him. On it he placed a bottle of *Nongtaegui*, an alcohol made with potatoes that my mother had given him, and that he'd held onto for a special occasion.

'Come, sit here,' he said to his brother Il-rok, pulling him by the arm. 'This is the coolest spot in the room.'

The four brothers, Il-seop, Seong-il, Il-rok et Myeong-sik, sat around the table and raised their glasses in a toast.

'*Keonbae!* (To your health!)' they said.

'Why were you sent so far away?' Great Uncle Il-seop whispered, infuriated. 'We haven't seen you for sixteen years! You've been completely unreachable. Do they separate families on purpose?'

'You know why,' Uncle Il-rok replied, sounding disillusioned. 'The more a family is divided, the less it is united. The State becomes your new family, it *replaces* your family.'

I didn't agree with what the adults had just said. The more a family is divided, I thought, the *more* it is united. Just look at me. I had been separated from my Aunt *Gomo* two years earlier and yet I had never missed her more than I did then. It was the opposite of what my uncle had said: distance brings families together.

Ah, *Gomo*. Where was she, anyway? What had become of her? And her boyfriend? That love story had forced *Halmeoni* to move out of the centre of Pukchong and into the suburb in the hope of putting an end to the rumours. The thought of *Gomo* stayed with me for the rest of the evening. I didn't dream then that I would not see her for another fifteen years, on the occasion of Little Uncle's wedding and then again after that, at *Unni*'s. Meanwhile, the three brothers emptied the bottle of *Nongtaegui*.

Uncle Il-rok left at the end of the evening. We never saw him again.

***

I must have been eleven years old when my father came home from work one day carrying a loaf of bread. Bread made from wheat flour, not corn or rice flour, it must have been quite expensive, costing at least 15 won. It was a gift from the *Galmaegi* restaurant in the port of Chongjin. My father had helped the place out with his tractor, and the manager of the restaurant had paid him in bread. Generally speaking, whenever we received such an unusual gift, we ate it in secret to avoid starting rumours and inciting the neighbours' envy. We could easily have been denounced had we not been careful. This story reminds me of one my father told me about my mother when she was pregnant with *Unni*. Knowing his wife did not have enough to eat, he came home from work one evening with a pot and went off to the river. He made a fire, took some rice from his pocket and cooked it, then brought it discreetly back to my mother. When I asked him why he'd gone down to the river to cook the rice, he explained that at the time there were many young couples, and they all suffered from malnutrition. He couldn't cook the rice at home because the neighbours would have smelled it and asked where he'd got it. *Bowibu*, the secret police, could have come to question him. My father admitted to us later that he had stolen a neighbour's shirts that had been hung out to dry and traded them for rice at the market. Our apartment was inspected many times, but not a trace of rice was found and no one ever got caught.

My mother sliced the bread into equal pieces and handed them out to us. It tasted so good, it was like swallowing honey. *Unni*, Jeong-ho and I were so delighted to have eaten this new delicacy, we talked about it all night. Of course, we couldn't tell anyone else about it. None of my friends could know – not Hye-rim, not Bok-soon.

***

Twice a month we got our rations card. People who worked received 700 or 800 grams of food each, depending on what their job was. Housewives got 300 grams and little children got 100. My mother and I both got 300 grams. Later, when I got to secondary school, I'd get 400 grams like my sister, and once we got to university – if we managed to get admitted – we'd get 600 grams each. I still remember that rations card: it was light pink. On it was our family's number, 256, the name of all our family members as well as what kind of food we would receive: corn, rice, tofu. Seventy per cent of the rations consisted of food made from corn.

There was another number, too: 419. That meant that we were to receive our rations on the 4th and 19th of the month. We eagerly awaited these magical days, because we knew that that evening there would be white rice on the table. Man, woman, child – we all had the same rice bowl and the same amount of rice in it. In some families the men got more, but in ours everyone was equal. When I think about it, my father was really a fair and respectable man. He was not at all like most other North Korean men, who preach equality but act macho in real life.

Every 4th and 19th of the month, my mother and sister took the card to the Public Distribution Centre five minutes from our flat. One day, my sister was sick and my mother asked me to go with her. The centre had two doors: one to go in and one to come out. We showed our card at the door so they could measure out what we had coming to us. Our card was handed to an official in the next room. We weren't allowed in there, but I could see what went on by looking through the tiny window in the booth where we waited. There were two metal buckets – one filled with corn, the other with rice. The officials carefully weighed the rice and the corn by hand, then poured the grains through a hole into a basin on the other side of the wall, in the room where I stood. We were not allowed to pick up any grains that fell on the floor. Sometimes the Public Distribution System allotted us noodles, but my brother and I didn't like that because they didn't fill us up – we always felt hungry right after eating them. On the way home, my mother carried our bag of rations on her back. That evening, the bag held a little rice, some corn and some salt. There was rarely soy sauce, sesame oil or sugar, and more rarely still any eggs. Those were for special occasions, such as the birthday of Kim Il-sung.

CHAPTER THREE

And when the rations were not enough to feed the family? You could try the Shop, if you had money. The only supermarket in the neighbourhood, it belonged to the government and was right across the street from our flat. It was really just a little stall where they only sold one thing at a time. When there was fish, for example, word would spread quickly among the *ajumma*: 'I saw the fish truck pull up! Hurry, let's go get in the queue at the Shop!' And in no time flat, a line of *ajumma* would form. Generally speaking, the merchandise was in the back of the stall, so from where I stood in line it was hard to see how much of it there was. When people had a feeling there wasn't enough for everyone, what had begun as an orderly queue would quickly be reduced to chaos. Adults, children, pregnant women … no one was spared. When you're eating to live, anything goes.

'Quit pulling my hair, you stupid bitch!'

'The next fish is mine! Get away!'

I hated going to the Shop but I'm the one my mother always sent – she knew I would never come home empty-handed.

***

My parents always carried a canvas bag with them in case they happened upon some food. One summer's day my mother came home with a bag full of peaches. I can still see *Unni*, my little brother and me jumping for joy over these mysterious fruits. I had never tasted them before. They were juicy and full of unknown flavours. I held the pit in my mouth, refusing to spit it out while I sucked the last bit of flavour from it. I agreed to spit it out only when my mother promised to give me another peach straight away. Once the peaches were eaten I made up a game to play with the pits.

My mother managed to give us such wonderful treats thanks to her small pig-raising business. She had worked tirelessly in order to stash away a little money so she could buy us these things. *We are so lucky*, I said to myself. *I bet Bok-soon has never tasted a peach!*

I revelled in such thoughts, even as I told myself over and over that I must never ask her the question.

In my mind, peaches will always be rare. They were grown mainly in Kimchaek (every city had its own fruit; in Ranam, for example, we grew pears) and a little bit in Pukchong, but those were not as good. I had no idea that I would have to wait twenty more years before seeing another peach – and that would be in China.

CHAPTER FOUR

'What would you like to drink?'

'Jihyun, what'll you have? I'm going to order a coffee.'

Sitting at our usual table at the back of the London's Victoria Place Café Rouge, we watch as the waitress pours the coffee into our cups. She places a sugar bowl on the table and gives us a beautiful smile before striding off. The coffee is delicious – strong and full of flavour. We like coming here. It's convenient, because Jihyun arrives at Victoria Coach Station whenever she comes down from Manchester. She takes the night coach – the train is too costly – but she is always ready to work at 8am sharp.

The station is constantly crowded with travellers rushing in all directions, but in the Café Rouge we can sit and talk, without having to think too much about the respective ideologies we were raised with. In these moments of calm, our lives come together – we cling to the things which draw us close rather to those that divide us. Jihyun spoons two teaspoons of sugar into her cup. She's starting to like the taste of coffee, but the first time I got her to try it she said she'd never take it without sugar. Always two teaspoons.

I listen as she tells me the story of her childhood. Nostalgia softens her face. I spend almost two hours feverishly taking notes as I struggle mightily to get her to talk about her day-to-day life as a young girl. It can be painstaking. I barely manage to find out what she wore as a girl. She remembers only that the top was white and the bottoms were black, that is all. *Her memories are in black and white*. It's an amazing detail, and I write it down in my notebook and put a star beside it. *Important*.

It occurs to me that nothing in her experience resembles mine, but simply by listening to what she shares with me I can place myself in her skin. I hear and feel every word, every sentence. I can still hardly make sense of the fact that this woman – so different yet so strangely familiar – used to live on the other side of the border, in that land the world had forgotten and which for me was synonymous with hell.

'Your childhood in the country reminds me of my own, you know,' I say, raising my head.

'It does?' she replies, intrigued.

'The kitchen a step down from the rest of the house, the big pot with the black metal lid that served as a stove, the "*ondol*" system for heating the floor – that's exactly how it was at my paternal grandparents' house out in the country. And then there's the fact that you called your grandmother *Halmeoni*, just as I called mine *Halmeoni*. It's almost as though sharing this language bridges the distance between us. Words like "*Halmeoni*" are like sudden bursts of life: they fly right to the heart.'

'Did you visit your grandparents often?' Jihyun asks, smiling a little sheepishly as if to say, *I get to ask questions, too!*

I'm a very private person. I don't go around telling people my life story. Sharing feelings doesn't come easily to me but I owe her an answer.

'Yes, when I was a child. My parents and I spent Christmas and summer vacations there. But as I got older, we visited less and less because we were living abroad. My father was a diplomat.'

'A *what*?'

'A … diplomat,' I stammered. 'Why?'

Have I just said something I shouldn't have? Do I come from a world which is too distant, too different from hers? Have I hurt her feelings? It's so complicated, being sincere. Suddenly I'm uncomfortable, but I don't know where this feeling is coming from. It's beyond my control. I was born in the 'good' Korea and Jihyun in the 'bad' one. I couldn't do anything about that. War criminals had divided the country in two, and it was easiest to leave it at that: life stopped at the 38th parallel.

'Wow, your father must be a very important man!' says Jihyun, almost blushing with admiration. 'He worked for the government … I understand now why you hesitated before accepting to write this book. This must not be easy for you.'

But I don't answer: my silence confirms that I too am taking risks by engaging in this project. She thanks me with her eyes.

'And here I thought you were just an ordinary South Korean living in London,' she says, teasing me. 'In fact, you're like a North Korean *Baekdu Hyultong* – someone who comes from the same lineage as Kim Il-Sung!'

I like her sense of humour, it bolsters me.

'Not exactly,' I say. 'In South Korea you can become a diplomat if you pass the national exam. It's got nothing to do with social class, you just have to be smart and study hard. If anything, my father's a self-made man. At the age of fourteen – that must've been right before the war – he was the first person in his village to walk around with *The Times* under his arm. He was dead set on learning English and becoming a diplomat, he wanted to see the world.'

'At fourteen, *my* father enlisted in the army!'

'I remember,' I say.

I want to get back on the same page with Jihyun as quickly as possible; I search for the right words.

'Like my father, yours spent his life serving his country. They just went about it differently. Yours wasn't lucky enough to go to school, but in a way each man stayed true to his career his whole life.'

'That's true.'

We're both moved. A little stunned, even. For a moment we lose each other, separated by the incongruous paths our lives have taken until now.

'Where did your father grow up?' Jihyun asks.

'In the Southwest – Jeolla Province.'

'*Jeolla*? My father's father was from Jeolla, too! My grandmother told me so. He was a southerner, like you – and like Kim Il-sung's ancestors. They were from Jeolla as well!'

'Really?' I say, unable to hide my surprise. I had no idea. They never taught us that in school. As a matter of fact, unless you are doing research on North Korea, I would be surprised if there are many out there who know about it. This discovery awakens in me an urgent desire to delve back into Korean history and drag these unknown facts and characters out into the light again.

'But to get back to your father, how many brothers and sisters did he have?' pursues Jihyun.

'Two brothers and a sister. My father was the youngest son, but he carried many family responsibilities, including financial ones.'

'Oh, I understand that,' says Jihyun, nodding. 'Mine, too. My grandmother's funeral was barely finished when he invited his two brothers to come live with us.'

'All his adult life, my father sent part of his salary home to his parents in the countryside. They lived in a house with a thatched roof. With the money he sent they were able to have their roof tiled. In the seventies that symbolised wealth! I remember being so sad when I arrived at my grandparents' house to find the thatched roof gone, replaced by hideous tiles. They clashed with the landscape. It was like a chapter of my childhood had been torn to pieces before my eyes. I didn't understand why getting richer meant making things uglier – it should have been the opposite.'

'But wait – for me, thatched roofs only exist in pictures! Like in the photo of the house in which Kim Il-sung was born. I've always lived in flats. The one house I ever knew was my grandmother's, and hers had a tiled roof!'

'Clearly, North Korea was wealthier than South Korea in the seventies,' I say, somewhat put out. And here I'd always believed that South Korea had always been rich and North Korea had always been poor! It's hard for me to digest this new version of history. It bothers me. I make a mental note to ask my father about it.

Jihyun and I look at each other in silence. Are we products of artificially generated differences?

'You know, you don't have an accent when you speak Korean – I mean a northern accent. I didn't dare ask you about it before, but it's intrigued me for a long time now,' I say.

'I know. I've worked hard not to – I didn't want to be looked down upon or discriminated against. Whenever I would meet someone from South Korea, I would pay close attention to the accent. Between escaping from North Korea and meeting you I've met a fair number of South Koreans – some in China, some in London at the human rights conferences I've attended. I wanted to be like other people. I guess you could call it a sort of survival instinct.'

'Did it take a lot of practice?' I ask.

'Not really. I'm fairly good at languages. Compared to what I went through to learn Chinese really fast, this was nothing.'

'How did you find the first South Koreans you met in England?'

'I was so surprised when they told me they were free to travel to different countries and live anywhere they wanted!' she says. 'That said, I didn't feel close to any of them right away. I still had too much hatred inside me, hatred I'd been trained to feel. It's not easy to get rid of that. Actually, to tell you the truth, you're the first South Korean I've ever trusted. I felt it during one of your visits to Manchester, when I watched you play with my children.'

I'm moved by what she's told me; it's huge. But I have to contain my feelings. I am not here to talk about myself; besides, I don't display my emotions that easily.

'I, too, felt uneasy when we met on the set of the documentary,' I say as calmly as I can. 'But I immediately felt something else toward you, too. A sort of intimacy, as though you were my sister. I can't explain why. But yes, a sister from the North, whose face I was seeing for the first time. Right away, I felt close to you.'

Jihyun nods her head. She grasps the magic of the moment we've just shared, the importance of saying the words, such as 'trust' or 'sister', that shatter the silence we've both lived in all our lives.

'You and I grew up differently and the paths we followed led in opposite directions. But despite our differences, we found each other,' she says quietly, as if she did not want to break the ambient enchantment by speaking loudly.

CHAPTER FIVE

I have a good memory for numbers. Often I've remembered an event simply by hearing a date – 15 April 1912, also known as The Day of the Sun, is the birth date of Kim Il-sung, 21 April 1892 is his mother's, 9 September 1948 marks the founding of the Democratic Republic of North Korea, while 16 February 1942 is the day Kim Jong-Il, the Shining Star, was born. Even today, it's still the date itself that calls an event to mind, not the other way around. I began memorising dates as early as nursery school so *The Life of Kim Il-sung* – that volume bursting with dates, that bible printed on beautiful white paper, that book of my childhood – will at least have served some purpose. After all, it's doubtless because of that book that I have a form of hypermnesia!

In September 1979, I entered the high school for girls in Nam-Chongjin. I was eleven. Snow had come early that year, and a few days before school began, my little brother, Jeongho, and I ran out into the streets to build a snowman. 'Down with the Americans!' he cried in his three-year-old's voice as he poured hot water over the snowman's head. The snowman melted in fast motion as we watched, mute with awe. Then we burst out laughing.

On school days I rose at 5am. I was always first to get up. With my red scarf tied around my neck, dressed in black and white, I still faithfully studied the lessons of Kim Il-sung's revolutionary feats and continued to participate in sports and musical activities after school. But one thing was new: foreign languages. Take Russian – a revelation! I found this East Slavic language written in Cyrillic both fascinating and delightful. I also studied Hanja, the Sino-Korean characters which complemented the purely phonetic Korean alphabet, Hangul, by adding a semantic dimension.

The costs of a secondary education were covered by the State, as those of my primary education had been. Now, in high school, there were enough textbooks for everyone, so our mothers didn't have to make us photocopies as they had before. That said, we still had to pay for them and many of my classmates couldn't afford to do so. I was one of the lucky ones who could buy a new book every year, so at the end of each school year I donated mine to the less fortunate students.

Cleaning the classrooms and toilets took on new meaning as well. Now we waxed our desks and cement floors with candles. That's why I always had a small rag in the drawer of my desk: whenever we took a short break, I'd take it out, give my desk a rub and *voilà*! The toilets were located outside, separate from the school building, and the job of cleaning them went to whoever had been denounced during the self-criticism sessions. Thankfully, this never included me. If farmers from the area hadn't come by regularly to collect our droppings for fertiliser, the toilets would have easily overflowed, especially in summer when it rained a lot. Then, everything would mix together – rain, excreta, mud. Winter was just as bad. A giant puddle of waste would freeze right in front of the doorway. To clear it, a team of students would have to hack away at it with pickaxes.

What was truly new in high school, though, was our trips to the countryside every semester. At harvest time, the collective farms would ask for help and the schools would supply them with a workforce of unpaid seasonal farm labourers: us students. These excursions looked less like children going on a picnic than young goats being herded by their Shepherdess-Teacher. And instead of grazing, we worked the soil with our clumsy little hands.

Each April, we'd leave home for about forty days. If there was weeding to be done, or if we didn't finish planting the rice, we stayed longer. In October, when we were sent to help harvest rice and corn, we were only gone for about two weeks.

CHAPTER FIVE

At thirteen, I went on my first forced-labour expedition to the countryside in 1981. One pleasant afternoon in September we were sent from Ranam to Orang, a city located an hour by train. In Orang, the farms produced mainly rice or corn. Our entire class, including our teacher, had been called up. There were thirty-six of us girls, all so excited by our first train ride. We laughed and messed around the entire way. We sped past village after village, and on the other side of the mountain we found ourselves in a world of rice paddies, dirt roads and rustic houses just like *Halmeoni*'s, with white walls and grey-tiled rooftops. All along these endless roads, giant letters rose up at intervals, inciting the people to grow rice with a warrior spirit:

« 모두다 가을걷이 전투에로»
'LET US HARVEST AS WE WOULD GO INTO BATTLE.'

Cooperative farms lined the road. Ploughs and carts were pulled by oxen or, in some more fortunate cases, by tillers. We saw a few Soviet-style tractors, too, though they were rare. Although my sister *Unni* had warned me that this excursion would be very difficult, I wasn't afraid – I was much stronger than she was and had done a lot of manual labour like this around Ranam. But this trip turned out to be nothing like the others. This time, the seven classes that made up our year were pitted against each other. Teacher told us we absolutely had to be the best. My parents had warned me that it wouldn't be safe to go out at night, but they hadn't said anything about how gruelling the physical work would be – they hadn't experienced anything like this when they were young. My mother helped me pack my bag. In it we put a change of clothes, a bit of salt, some soap and a toothbrush. She also gave me some grilled corn and a bit of cornflour, which I could make into a paste by adding a little water.

When we got to the station in Orang, we piled out of the train and set off on foot. Walking briskly, we arrived at the farm by mid-afternoon, but no one was there – everyone was in the fields. All we could do was wait outside the farmer's office until somebody came by. *Hurray, we've got free time!* I thought to myself excitedly. The Orang River was right before us. Teacher was basking in the sun, and when we started playing in the river she didn't stop us. Even though Ranam was only forty minutes from the sea and the Rabook River ran close to our house, that was the first time I ever went swimming. I'd never gone in the Rabook. It wasn't safe: the bottom had been dredged for sediment to use in building construction, and that had created a dangerous current. Many people had drowned there and our parents strictly forbade us from going near it.

But the waters of the river in Orang were calm, and we could touch the bottom. We splashed and played like there was no tomorrow. None of us knew how to swim, but we didn't care – this was our first time swimming and that was exciting enough. In the midst of all the horseplay, the screams of Hyang-sook and Hae-young got us even more keyed up.

'A snake!' they shrieked at the tops of their lungs.

'Help!' we howled, panicking. 'Let's get out of here!'

'You're so silly,' someone said. 'That's not a snake, it's a trout!'

'Oh, wow, look at that! It's got a rainbow on its back, it's so pretty!'

Teacher watched the whole thing without even scolding us; she just let us play. She looked a little uneasy, even anxious, like someone who found herself in a completely new situation and didn't quite know what to do. We students, though, were quick to laugh. At thirteen, life was good …

A few hours later, the farmer finally came in from the fields. He and Teacher agreed on how to divvy up the chores and who would sleep where. We were each assigned to a host family and paired off a bit randomly, but I was lucky enough to room with my artistic friend In-hee, the one who was good at drawing and whose mother made amazing paper flowers. The house we stayed in belonged to a single woman more or less my mother's age; she was very kind and gentle. She gave us a blanket and a mattress, but no food. We didn't complain, though – some girls had to sleep directly on the floor!

The next morning we expected to be sent to the fields, but the farmers kept us there to clean the corn, beans, radishes and cabbage. Once the corn was harvested, it was our job to husk each ear and then remove the kernels. Our young fingers weren't strong enough to separate the tightly packed kernels, and the golden corn would soon be stained with a mixture of blood and pus. We weren't allowed to chat, we could only whisper to each other when we were sure Teacher didn't hear. We would suck on the husk that enveloped each ear of corn. Its sweet juice tasted delicious. Most of the time, we worked under the farmer's watch, with Teacher nowhere in sight. We had no idea where she went. During these corn-husking excursions to the countryside, we stopped having our lessons, but the daily self-criticism sessions never stopped.

On the way to the fields, we picked radishes that grew along the path. Long, slender and white, they were unlike anything you ever saw in the city. I don't know if it was hunger or the fact that they were forbidden that made them taste so good or if they really *were* that good, but we gobbled them down. We got caught, of course, and we were punished, but we were hungry. We could withstand the punishment if it meant we had a little something in our stomachs. The supplies we'd brought in our bags hadn't lasted more than ten days.

Unni was right after all: the physical work was brutal and exhausting. I cried every night in the dark before falling asleep. We all did. We were only thirteen years old and overcome with fatigue; even talking was too much effort. It was a relief just to let the tears flow in the silent darkness, mourning together and yet alone. I missed home in Ranam, and I missed *Halmeoni*'s house too, where the neighbours gathered to laugh and tell jokes. In this village, the farmers worked so hard they didn't even have the strength to smile, much less chat with neighbours. Here, the children cried themselves to sleep.

***

Thanks to my good grades and popularity, I became class delegate that same year, in 1981. I headed up a team of three sub-delegates, each of whom was in charge of a group of girls and responsible for supervising their homework sessions. As for me, I was responsible for the daily self-criticism sessions. I gave Teacher the names of the students who were denounced and also sent them to do their penance of cleaning the outdoor toilets. It was hugely stressful – I had to be on guard constantly lest anyone play a dirty trick on me. I hid behind the notion that I was 'doing my duty', and carried out my tasks calmly and without remorse.

My high school years were spent working. On Sundays when I wasn't called to school for some physical chore, I'd spend the whole day studying for tests. During holidays, I would often coordinate with Soon-hee, In-ok and Jung-gum to help each other out with homework.

Paper was in very short supply so we couldn't afford to waste it. Except for *The Life of Kim Il-Sung*, all our textbooks and workbooks were printed on crude brown paper and it was all but impossible to write in them. One day, my father came home from working in a paper factory in Kilju, and with a needle and thread he sewed sheets of paper together into a notepad we could write on. The paper he'd brought back to us was of such poor quality it felt like writing on wood but at least it was paper. My classmates weren't as lucky.

In order to take part in national holidays such as the birthdays of Kim Il-sung and Kim Jong-Il, we had to undergo intense choral training after school in preparation for a concert. I didn't care for singing all that much and I always got away by reciting poetry instead. There was also a gymnastics competition we had to enter each spring, after we returned from the countryside. By then we were so exhausted from the physical labour we could barely walk, but we had to suffer through splits and other acrobatic feats for three or four hours every day after school. We were never home before eight in the evening. Our class always finished near the top, but at what price?

CHAPTER FIVE

One spring when I was still fourteen, we went on our second trip to the country, this time to the city of Saebyul. Now known as Kyungwon Koon, the city is located north of Chongjin in the far north-eastern part of the Korean Peninsula, near the border with China. I couldn't know then how many springs and autumns I would end up spending there. The journey from Chongjin was not an easy one. We had to change trains twice and always arrived either in the middle of the night or very early in the morning, which meant we never had the chance to get to know the scenery surrounding Saebyul. Our work consisted of taking rice seedlings from a clearly marked plot and transplanting them in the rice paddy, being sure they were well submerged. We were given a wooden stool to sit on from time to time, but there was never a moment to use it. Each of us had to complete a plot about 5 metres long and almost 2 metres wide before breakfast, and we couldn't afford to take one minute to sit down. It was cold at daybreak, even in springtime. We didn't have warm clothing, and our hands and feet were constantly frozen. If one of us failed to finish planting his plot the others would try to help, but we were so exhausted that we were barely able to lend a hand. And of course, whoever didn't finish was denounced during the daily self-criticism session. Thankfully, I was a fast worker and always finished my quota on time.

Meal times were always the most painful. All that was left from the supplies that our parents had packed in our bags was some soy sauce, soy paste and pickled radishes, but whoever was assigned to prepare the meal was a lucky girl! One day it was my turn to grind corn to make corn meal and also make noodles. I spent the whole day bent over the pasta roller and my back was killing me, but putting up with the pain was worth it.

'You may take some of this back to your room and share it with your friends,' said Teacher.

'Really?' I asked.

'Be discreet. Go now, take some and get out of here!'

That was one of those times when I knew that all my efforts to become the teacher's pet had paid off. Necessity triumphed over morality and I gave in instantly, choosing to be pragmatic rather than question her gesture. Why didn't I rebel? It never crossed my mind. Building up one's resilience or even a sense of 'collusion with the enemy' was more important than revolution.

One day we were working in the fields near the Tumen River, which separates North Korea from China on its eastern border. We could see the fields on the other side but we never saw anyone working in them. It was strange. Our teacher didn't offer any explanation for this and we didn't ask questions, but we knew that it was another world over there. The way the houses looked and the style of clothing were different: it was China. Oddly, we noticed that the fields were covered in giant sheets of black plastic.

'Those Chinese,' I whispered. 'They're so lazy. No one's even working in the fields.'

'They've got a strange way of growing crops, that's for sure,' In-hee replied.

'Do you think they know how to farm the land without getting their hands dirty like us?' I asked.

'Pffft, what a bunch of clowns! I don't know what's going on under there, but they're stupid. Bunch of lazybones. Look how hard we work, they could never keep up with us!' she said disdainfully before getting back to work.

Sometimes a few Chinese would come down to the river to wash their clothes. They would stare at us and we would stare right back. We were barely 20 metres apart, but no one spoke. We had nothing to say to each other – a mere 20 metres was all it took to keep the two worlds apart.

***

Could *Juche* have explained this difference? At a very young age we became accustomed to relying only on ourselves. A spirit of resistance born during the Japanese occupation, *Juche* means 'to count on one's own strengths', that is, to favour absolute autonomy and thereby become the master of one's own destiny. This notion of self-reliance extended to economic and military realms, as well, and also to family life. You had to learn to manage alone. Get yourself to the meeting place with Teacher alone when you're six years old. Do your homework alone. When the rest of the family is busy, play alone. This instilled in us an incredible strength of character but with no room for emotions to develop. Yet when I think back on this time, I'm filled with a profound sorrow. It saddens me to think that my parents could not afford to play with their children the way I am able to do with mine.

***

The year 1982 also marked another event as well: on Kim Jong-Il's fortieth birthday, his portrait was allowed to appear alongside his father's. Some schools had to wait years before the government sent them one, but our school was among the first to acquire The Portrait, and we were very proud indeed.

Between the homework and the competitions, our high school lives were so regulated that there wasn't much time for frivolity. Except for this one day in October 1983, when we were fifteen years old. Some of my friends from the neighbourhood came running to find me.

'They're handing out apples for free in the orchards!' they exclaimed, breathless.

No sooner had we heard the words than Soon-hee, In-ok, Jung-gum and I ran to fetch some grey cloth sacks, then headed for the hill. It was a steep climb to Gudeok and before too long we were out of breath. There were lots of people at the orchard. They had volunteered to collect the rotten apples that had fallen on the ground. In return, they would be given fresh apples at the end of the day. Children weren't allowed to take part, so we pretended to play nearby, picking up leaves. When the farmer had his back turned, we ran towards a tree, quickly swiped some apples from the branches and hid them in our bags. Getting caught would have meant being punished during a self-criticism session. We ran as fast as we could, feeling safe only once we had climbed into the highest branches of the apple tree. From our perch high on that hill in Gudeok, we gazed out at the little villages with their one- and two-storey buildings of red brick, at the fields, at the orchards. Sitting on the branches, we set about enjoying our loot at last – only to discover that the apples were far too hard for our young teeth to bite into: they were inedible.

'What a scam!' I cried, outraged.

'All that for nothing,' Soon-hee and In-ok grumbled.

'Now I know why that farmer had a crafty smile on his face when he talked to us. What a jerk!'

Furious, I didn't say a word the whole way home.

***

My anger that day was only made worse by the unbearable smell that attacked my nostrils as I approached my neighbourhood. It wasn't the first time I'd seen whitings drying on balconies – and in fact, I found the stinky fish delicious – but that day their odour of smelly feet infuriated me: why did everyone have to set their fish out to dry? Why?

And then there was the 'Dormitory for 3,000', a block of flats recently built by soldiers who had completed their military service. Some 3,000 more people in the neighbourhood, almost overnight – you couldn't help but notice them. In the evenings they all came home at the same time from the steel plant in Chongjin where they worked. We could hear them coming by their thundering steps, and we knew better than to be in the vicinity during rush hour or we'd drown in a tide of men. They seemed unremarkable, but my father had warned us: they were hungry and they stole.

CHAPTER FIVE

I was sick and tired of constantly being in a state of high alert. It was exhausting. Planting corn all day in the fields, collapsing every evening without washing (or even wanting to), lacking the strength even to crawl under the blanket, feeling the cracked skin of my palms from handling the stalks of corn while the sun burned my face and chapped my lips, suffering this drudgery day after day, only to have to contend with the noise of pigs and the stench of dried fish and the hordes of soldiers in the streets as I made my way home. Did this serve any purpose? Was it normal?

And then there were the silkworms. The government had ordered every family to breed them – to become sericulturists, in short – and contribute to the nation's textile production by donating the cocoons. This became one more responsibility for the building's *ajummas*. The eggs were barely the size of black sesame seeds. You had to place them on damp mulberry leaves to get them to hatch. After they did, the worms would eat the leaves, growing and growing ... We needed so many leaves my mother ended up bringing entire branches back from the mountains and placing them in a pot in the corner of the room. Sleeping under those branches felt like camping out under the open sky. In the night, the white worms would fall on our heads like snowflakes. When we woke, the mushy, cylinder-shaped creatures with their jointed legs would be everywhere. My arms and neck and face would be crawling with them, and I'd pluck them off mechanically, neither disgusted nor annoyed. At least the little caterpillars weren't bothersome; they didn't make any noise and they didn't smell bad. Our cohabitation – and our duty – ended the day they encased themselves in a cocoon. Once the cocoons were formed, we sent them to factories where they'd be boiled, unravelled, and spun. The silk thread would then be used to make textiles for export.

***

Every day at five in the morning, I went to the stream. The only quiet place I knew, it was a little nameless stream near our flat where my mother did the washing. It was the perfect place for me to work out my maths problems and memorise the History of the Revolution, both of which required a good deal of concentration: one wrong date could cost you your future. We were all maths buffs in our family, especially my sister *Unni*. She used to compete in computer programming contests. There was no computer for her in school, but they did give her a pretend keyboard made just for her so she could learn to type. The keys were actually the black caps from paint tubes on which the Korean vowels and consonants had been written in white, and the caps were mounted on a plastic box. She brought that keyboard home every evening and practised, her fingers flying over the keys as though she were playing a piano, only muted. Then she would fill her workbook with mathematical formulae. Although she had never touched a computer, she could write programs. She even told me she knew how to create an image of the Korean flag waving in the wind. In 1983 she won second place for computer programming at a competition in Bulyeong in North Hamgyong Province. That same year, Jeong-ho, who was now six, started school – he was good at maths, too, just like us.

***

One summer's day in 1984, the general secretary of the Communist Party of China, Hu Yaobang, came to Chongjin. That year we were studying Chinese in school, so I was very interested in his visit. I knew Korea and China were blood brothers because China had helped us during the Korean War and that my mother had distant relatives in China. Occasionally, I watched Chinese films on neighbours' television sets, but beyond that my knowledge of the country was very limited: *Do the Chinese look like us?* I wondered. *Do they eat like us? Do they live like us?*

That day, everyone lined up along the wide central avenue called Route 2 to watch the parade. The people of Ranam were accustomed to this kind of demonstration. Loudspeakers blasted unintelligible instructions while security guards blew their whistles at you so loudly your eardrums almost burst. Everyone moved quickly, but without knocking each other over or complaining. The entire city of Ranam, whose population numbered in the hundreds of thousands, assembled in less than forty-five minutes. Those with the best *songbun* (class) had the honour of standing at the front of the crowd. Because we were schoolchildren, we were told to stand near the middle. We waved our little Chinese and Korean flags while shouting at the tops of our lungs, 'Welcome General Secretary and Kim Il-sung!' at the large black car they were riding in. My father managed to catch a glimpse of Dear Leader but my mother, whose *songbun* was lower than my father's, had been placed so far back she couldn't see a thing.

Back at home, my father toasted his good spirits with a glass of liquor that he made from corn and kept for happy occasions. He enjoyed a little drink from time to time. That evening, he told us how proud he was to be a member of the Party. At one point, he stood and went to the cupboard where he kept his red-cloth wallet under the pile of neatly folded clothes. He withdrew a folded red card: « 조선 노동당 당원증 ». On the front it said, 'Card of the Workers Party of Korea'. On the inside was a photo of him and the date he had joined. I'd long been aware that my father kept something important hidden in the cupboard, but that was the first time he revealed what the treasure was. I think that card meant more to him than his own life, so it went without saying that he cherished it more than he did us. And that made complete sense to me.

'I hope that you will have your own someday,' he said, waving his card around.

Suddenly, in one swift movement, he raised his shirt and showed us something totally unexpected: a huge scar on the left side of his lower belly. For a moment we were all speechless.

'In 1959, near the end of my military service in Kangwondo,' he told us, 'I captured a South Korean spy!'

'Where is Kangwondo?' Jeong-ho asked, intrigued.

'It's a province that shares a border with South Korea. I was on duty on Mount Kumgang. It was a strategic post, given its proximity to the South.'

'And? Then what happened?' *Unni* asked impatiently.

'I spotted the spy and I threw myself on him.'

'How did you do it? From behind? From the front? Did you have a gun?' Jeong-ho wanted to know.

'No need for you to know the details,' my father said abruptly. 'There are military secrets I can't share with you. What I can tell you is that as we were fighting he knifed me in the gut and I lost consciousness. When I woke up, not only was I still alive, but I had been made *Hwason Iptang* – a member of the Party – on the spot because I had killed the spy. I was a war hero!'

'*Abeoji choego*,' we cried. 'You're the best! We are so proud of you!'

My father was barely twenty-two years old when that happened. Mum told us how proud of him she was. I was, too, of course, but I never spoke of this with my friends. Some of them had parents who were both Party members, while only my father was. I didn't want to talk about my mother – I was ashamed of her.

CHAPTER SIX

I'd always known my mother was lower class. While that hadn't bothered me too much, I did often wonder why my father had married someone with a bad *songbun*. He had done ten years of exemplary military service. He had captured a South Korean spy on Mount Kumgang and, hey presto, been made a member of the Party. He was a war hero! So why hadn't he married a war *heroine*, someone of his rank?

One day in late 1984 when I came home from school, Mum decided it was time to explain the situation to us. We had just got the news that my sister had not been awarded the research position in the army she'd applied for, despite having won first place in a computer programming contest. *Unni* was really good in school. Not only class delegate, she was head of our school's board of delegates. She had spent her whole life working to be eligible for that job, she had even got herself a military uniform – she'd modelled it for me in secret one day before carefully returning it to the cupboard.

Yet despite these efforts, this model student and model daughter had just been rejected by the Party. Deeply dismayed by the news, she spent the evening shut up in the toilet crying. Our father, who had until then been a firm believer in *juche* (self-reliance), resorted to drinking to hide his disappointment. Mum had a hard time masking her discomfort, but she didn't say a word about it that evening. It wasn't until the next day that she spoke up. Waiting for us at the door, she was trembling, her eyes wet with tears.

'Children …' she began.

My heart stopped. I understood this was very serious.

'Gather round,' she said, 'and promise me you won't repeat a word of what I'm about to tell you.'

We had barely put down our schoolbags.

'I promise,' said *Unni* dutifully.

'I must tell you something about our family. It's very important.'

'What about our family?' I stammered, overwhelmed with a feeling of foreboding.

'Your father and I were married in spite of our difference in social rank. My *songbun* is not pure. Your father had to lie to *Halmeoni*. He told her I was a member of the Communist Party so she would allow the marriage. He presented me as someone who had managed to become a member of the Communist Party, thanks to my exceptional work in the factory. He told her my parents were dead. You see, at the time, every future mother-in-law in the village wanted her son or daughter to marry a member of the Party.'

'But why did he lie?' Jeong-ho asked, puzzled.

'So that *Halmeoni* would give us permission to get married. She wouldn't have wanted your father to marry someone of a lower rank.'

'He lied to his mum for you,' I said, moved.

'Your father is a responsible son, and pragmatic too. He wanted to marry someone who could take care not only of him but of his aged mother, his handicapped brother and his youngest brother as well. A woman of his *songbun* would never have accepted to take so much on. That meant he needed a woman from a lower class, because she would be grateful to reach a higher rank through marriage and so would spend the rest of her life dedicated to her husband's family.'

I tried to meet *Unni*'s gaze. Even if we knew it was not our place to demand explanations when it came to this topic, we also knew we could no longer back away from difficult questions. *Unni* looked at me approvingly, so I dared to ask,

'But why is your *songbun* inferior? Don't you come from a good family?'

'Your grandfather, my father, defected to the South during the war.'

I couldn't believe my ears. I was crushed. It couldn't be! This couldn't be happening to us. Not to the Parks. We were a perfect family, we had never done anything wrong. My father was a war hero. We had always been good students. Our maternal grandparents were dead – or at least that's what we thought. It's why we never talked about them.

'So he was a *Banyeokja*?' I asked, distraught.

'Let me explain,' my mother said sternly. Her tone contained none of the tenderness of before; it was devoid of emotion. 'My father owned land in Kimchaek during the Japanese occupation. His name was Taewoo Rho. After the liberation in 1945 he tried to join the Communist Party, but there was no place in the Party for a former landowner corrupted by capitalism. Then, during the Korean War, sometime between 1950 and 1953, he decided to try his luck in the South. In the North, he would only ever be a downgraded capitalist with no future. One day he asked my mother to pack their bags and be ready to leave that evening, but when the time came she didn't have the courage to go with him so my father defected alone. My mother gave me to my Uncle Tae-sop, and then she too disappeared. She was barely twenty years old.'

Mom went on to explain that Uncle Tae-sop, furious that my grandmother had abandoned his niece, went searching for her all over Chongjin. Eventually he found her, but she refused to take her daughter back – she didn't want her.

'What?' Jeong-ho whispered. He was shaking. 'Your mother abandoned you?'

'Yes. She wanted nothing to do with my father's family, the Rhos.'

A husband who defected to the South would attract attention. My mother's mother was afraid for her brothers and sisters, so she chose to run away. She knew that if she lived in hiding for a few years, her case would be automatically classified as a divorce and that she would no longer be tainted by her husband's treason: she would no longer be a deserter's wife.

'But that was so selfish of her!' I exclaimed, beside myself. 'How could she abandon her own child? And *Halabeoji*, how could he go alone and leave his wife and child behind?'

I tried to keep calm because I didn't want the neighbours to hear, but I was furious. I was starting to hate my maternal grandparents even though I had never met them: they were traitors, both of them. I could understand that my father would lie to his mother to be able to marry the woman he loved, but I could not forgive my grandparents for abandoning their family to save their own skin.

'Wait a second – if my grandfather defected, does that make me the granddaughter of a southern barbarian?'

'I'm sorry.'

I don't know if it was anger or survival instinct, but my mind wandered. My grandmother had abandoned my mother. Still, I knew that the Party came first, even when it was a question of your own child. A few years ago, a young mother had died in a fire, clutching a portrait. *The* Portrait. Her baby died too, but The Portrait survived. The story made the front page of the newspapers: the woman had chosen to save The Portrait and not her baby. The consequence of her heroic death was a blessed future for her husband and their other children: they would have Kim Il-Sung's protection for three generations to come. Abandoning my mother was my grandmother's way of remaining true to the Party, I said to myself. Her heroic act had simply been to rid herself of a deserter's child: first, the Party, then the child.

Now *Unni* understood why she hadn't been given the army job: it was because the tainted blood of a deserter's child – our mother – ran through her veins.

'I want to do everything in my power to keep this family secret hidden,' my mother said. 'To do that, you must simply act as if nothing's amiss. If anyone asks you questions about your maternal grandfather, tell them your grandfather is dead and that for you your grandfather has always been Tae-sop, just as you've done until now. Do you understand?'

I would have loved for my sister to interrupt Mum, to tell her to stop talking about Uncle Tae-sop. I wanted her to say, 'Uncle Tae-sop can't help get me that position! You know full well it's because of you I didn't get it.' But *Unni* was too reserved, such words would never come out of her mouth – 'God only knows what's going on inside her,' my mother used to say when *Unni* would shut down.

Our maternal grandfather died on our mother's tongue that afternoon. As we looked at each other silently, we didn't really know what to do with the word that had just invaded our lives: I, Jihyun, sixteen years old, member of the *Sonyundan*, was descended from a *deserter*. If my schoolmates found out, they would surely tell everyone and bully us. The truth must never come out, I simply must not be the granddaughter of a deserter.

Was it anger I felt towards my mother? Was it pity? Everything was mixed up in my head. It was only later that I learned she had had a difficult childhood. Orphaned, brought up by her Uncle Tae-sop in Chongjin, she had spent her entire childhood being resented by her Aunt Sung-ok for the bad *songbun* she'd dragged into the family. He aunt called her a *ssangnyon*, or whore. It was *ssangnyon* this, *ssangnyon* that. Until she met my father, Mum had a terrible time overcoming the label 'Daughter of a Deserter'. In some ways, I was happy for her that she found some relief, thanks to him. But what about us? Weren't we the grandchildren of a deserter, without having done anything? And what might our mother do to *us*? Would she abandon us one day, if she felt she was in danger? Was it self-interest or survival instinct that had made her father leave? I understood now why *Halmeoni* would never have accepted her as a daughter-in-law if my father hadn't lied about her social standing.

***

Thanks to our secret-keeping, my family's status, now tainted by my grandfather's desertion, didn't affect me that year. The only pressure on me had to do with my grades at school. I could not afford to fail Revolutionary History. The other subjects, like World History, didn't matter – they weren't graded. But I needed to excel on my final exam in Revolutionary History if I was to go to university. Driven by the terror of failure, I devoted myself to my studies with supreme diligence. I was very ambitious and dreamed of attending University of Pyongyang. That for me was the ultimate destination, the way to become part of the 'elite'.

We spent a lot of time studying Party philosophy that year. Kim Jong-Il had just written a work called *The Idea of Juche*. Though the philosophy of *juche* was introduced under Kim Il-sung in 1955, Kim Jong-Il's book was not published until 1982. According to him, we were a chosen people and the masters of our own destiny. He was our leader, he would show us the way. Everyone – from *ajumma* in the home to fathers at work – had to learn the philosophy by heart. At the time there were no photocopiers, but I ensured we had a copy *The Idea of Juche* at home by transcribing it by hand, in black ink, on paper that my father had set aside carefully for our homework. The book was placed on a shelf in the main room, next to about twenty other books, all of them about Kim Il-sung. I had never seen this hero in the flesh but I was in awe of him and his family – I knew I owed them more respect than I owed my own parents.

At sixteen, having good grades was not simply a matter of memorising *The Idea of Juche*. You also had to have great oratory skills, reciting the text out loud with the utmost eloquence and just the right intonation. During parent – teacher meetings, the teachers would read their comments aloud to the parents. The names of the best students were prominently displayed on the wall at eye level. Thankfully, *Unni*, Jeong-ho and I were always among them. That made my parents very happy, but when they complimented us we always had a feeling that they thought we could do even better.

CHAPTER SIX

Every day was like the day before it: we worked, washed the windows, painted the walls of the school buildings, went to gather wood, learned to shoot a handgun – after all, war might break out at any moment and we had to be ready. The only novelty was my new friend, Hye-young Chi. A poor pupil, she was always being scolded by Teacher during the weekly self-criticism sessions. Seeing her get upset and burst into tears pained me so much, I offered to help her with her homework and her revision. Without realising it, I was following in the footsteps of my sister *Unni*, who had done the exact same thing for me.

As far as the school was concerned, I was 'Myeong-sil's sister' before I was Jihyun. In a certain way I found that flattering. One day, Myeong-sil came home with a maths book that she too had copied by hand. I knew there was only one copy available at school and that she had gone to a lot of trouble to be able to help me at home. It was a kind and generous gesture, and I was deeply touched. I am still certain today that I became good at maths thanks to her, to her devotion and her gesture of kindness, for which she asked nothing in return.

Little by little, Hye-young's grades improved thanks to our homework sessions, and this deepened our friendship as well. She was the eldest of four and her mother – an *ajumma*, like mine – gave her many chores to do around the house. Her father had been sent to Russia by the government three years earlier: you had to be a member of the Party and have really good *songbun* to be sent there.

'Your father works abroad!' I said admiringly one afternoon after we'd finished our homework. 'What does he do?'

'Erm, I don't know. He's never told me. All I know is he lives in Russia. And anyway, what he does is not really the important thing. What counts is that thanks to him, the government gave us a colour telly and lots of Russian-made notebooks and pencils! Imagine! His work must be very good for us to be compensated like that. In any case, I'm super proud of him.'

Before her father left for Russia, the National Security office had made her family sign a non-disclosure agreement, so Hye-young rarely spoke of him. I wished she would talk to me about the three years she spent without her father but the time was never quite right to ask her. We were extremely close and should have been able to confide in one another more, but what with non-disclosure agreements and fears of being denounced, it was difficult to achieve real intimacy even between the closest of friends.

Our lives were highly disciplined and commendable in every way, yet I couldn't help noticing that the ambience at home was getting worse and worse since my sister failed to get the army position. Our parents fought often. Did my father regret his decision not to marry someone of his rank? Was he angry with himself for not having realised in time that his children's lives would be affected? The least little thing had become a pretext for quarrelling.

'Myeong-sil *abeoji*, father of Myeong-sil, I can no longer get the rations we need. I have to fight for the least little piece of tofu,' my mother whinged one evening when my father came home from work.

'What are you talking about? Not enough rations? You have to fight for them? That's rubbish! The Party has assured me there's enough food for everyone. I don't want to hear about it,' he said loudly and walked out of the kitchen.

As though drinking could help him to forget his worries, he went to the bedroom and poured himself a glass. 'Now she can't even figure out the portions we're entitled to,' he muttered as he took his first sip of corn alcohol. 'On top of everything else, she's becoming lazy!'

Times were tough. It's true, my mother was more concerned with putting a bowl of rice on the table every day than cleaning the walls of our block of flats. But one evening when my father came home, instead of their usual row, I watched as he discreetly went to the kitchen. He was carrying a backpack made of black cloth the way you would cradle a baby. Thankfully, no one had seen him enter the building. All the *ajumma* were busy getting dinner ready, the corridors were empty. Still, he cast a furtive glance over his shoulder before closing the door of the flat just to be sure no one had seen him. Intrigued by this unusual behaviour, we all followed him, eager to find out what was in the backpack. He motioned to us to remain silent. Placing the backpack on the table, he withdrew fifty white eggs one by one and placed them carefully beside the backpack. Barely able to contain her excitement, Mum took the eggs in her hands, counting them over and over again before placing them in a large bowl. I couldn't take my eyes off those white shells – I'd never seen so many eggs in my life. I was dazzled.

After several moments, my mother broke the silence.

'Whatever will we do with them?' she whispered, worried.

'They're from a farm in Ranam. I got them in return for some work I did,' my father said. 'I know that normally I've no right to touch them since they belong to the State, but I couldn't say no.'

'So you took them illegally?' I asked in a shaky voice.

'That's right. And if any of our neighbours see or hear about this, they'll denounce us to the police and we'll be arrested immediately.'

As the four of us stood in the kitchen, our excitement soon turned to fear.

'But Daddy ...', stammered *Unni,* staring up at him.

'Boil them, all of them. Now! We're going to eat them all at once,' my father said, resolute. He had thought this through all the way home – no one must know he'd brought fifty eggs home to us. His face betrayed no emotion but his tone was firm:

'Do not speak of this beyond these walls. Tell no one that you've been eating eggs.'

Even though our neighbours usually knocked before coming in, my mother locked the door. We turned out the light. Mum put the eggs on to boil. We huddled together in the main room of the flat, where we waited for a good ten minutes – we could hear the eggs knocking against each other in the pot. Once they were cooked, Mum put them in a bowl and placed the bowl on the floor in a corner of the room.

'Ten each,' she said calmly.

The words had barely passed her lips when we rushed to devour our eggs – we were so hungry, it was worth the risk of getting caught. We ate in silence as though taking part in a sacred ceremony, as though the least little noise would ruin the taste. Jeong-ho, *Unni* and I exchanged happy glances with each new eggshell we cracked. More than once, my father placed a finger over his lips to remind us not to make a sound. He didn't need to, though – we all knew what would happen if Mrs Jang from next door overheard us.

Jeong-ho was the first to finish his eggs, and when *Unni* and I had finished ours, we simply stared at each other in a state of bliss, our bellies full. We would have sat there a long time like that, without moving, if my father had not broken the silence.

'The eggshells,' he said, sounding nervous, 'how do we get rid of them?'

The question caught us off guard. We sat there for several seconds, rooted to the spot. My father had planned his caper perfectly, from transporting the eggs to eating them, but he had forgotten to include a plan for getting rid of the evidence. Wide-eyed, we stared at our parents, willing them to hurry and find a solution.

'Let's grind them up in the mortar and throw the grounds in the fire!' said Mum, the pestle already in her hand before she'd got to the end of her sentence.

After several minutes, she had reduced the shells to a fine powder, which she sprinkled over the flames. She placed another log on the fire. No one would ever know: it was the perfect crime.

That feeling of eating my fill … I think that in the thirty-five years I lived in North Korea, I only experienced it twice. Once, when I was eight years old and my father brought bread back from a factory in Ranam, and the day I ate ten eggs in a row.

***

Nineteen eighty-four, the year I turned sixteen, was also the year my Uncle *Jagueun Abeoji* got married. His wife's name was Ok-soon

Hwang. My uncle was short and had tiny little eyes, but to my astonishment his bride was very pretty. She was tall, taller than he was, and older by three years. I thought they made an odd couple, but watching them smile at each other constantly led me to believe they were truly happy. The day of the wedding, despite the June heat, my uncle wore a black suit. Ok-soon Hwang wore a traditional Korean dress in pale pink. She carried a bouquet of flowers and, just above her low chignon, she wore paper flowers in her hair. My uncle too had paper flowers, in the pocket of his jacket. Pink paper flowers. To see them looking so lovely made me want to get married, too.

When someone from the *inminban* got married, it was the kids in the building who were most delighted of all. The families of the newlyweds would share the food that they prepared for the occasion, and the idea that we would soon eat our fill put us in a state for days leading up to the wedding. My mother went all out for the event, preparing rice cakes, *kwajul*, fried rice, fruits, a chicken, steamed fish and noodles. On the table she placed a tiered cake made of *shimt-teok*, or unsweetened rice cakes, another with pears and apples, and, in the middle, the chicken with a red chilli in its beak. For twelve months leading up to this day, Mum had had to set aside two teaspoons of rice from each bi-monthly ration so she would have enough for the feast – I'm sure that North Korean mothers are the only people in the world capable of performing such a feat!

Our neighbour, Mrs Jang, spent two whole days helping us prepare the food. My father, who loved large gatherings, happily invited all his friends as well as all my uncle's friends to celebrate together.

When the meal was over, we followed the couple to the enormous statue of Kim Il-sung in Chongjin. Placing flowers at the statue was required before the next step – recording the marriage at the police station. After the papers were signed at the Pohang station, we walked to the house where my Aunt *Gomo*, whom I hadn't seen in ten years, was waiting for us. She was twenty-seven years old then and the spitting image of my grandmother. That evening, my uncle drank with his friends in the main room. His wife waited patiently in the neighbour's flat, as was the custom – she could not remove her bridal gown until her husband gave her permission.

I had barely got over the void left by my Uncle *Jagueun Abeoji*'s parting when another event occurred to mark that summer: a public execution.

***

Jeong-ho, *Unni* and I had just come home from school when the *inmanbanjang* knocked on our door and told us to go back right away: a traitor had just been arrested and was about to be punished.

'This is a rare thing,' she said, and promptly disappeared.

We were a little confused by how suddenly everything was happening. Not only that, our parents had never really explained what 'punishing a traitor' meant. I knew some of my friends had already attended an execution, but this was our first.

As we hurried back to the school, we didn't dare look at each other or even talk. At school, Teacher lined us up class by class and led us to the Rabook River. The sky was low and heavy with clouds. The execution was to take place on the bridge, where the greatest number of people could gather and visibility was best. By the time we arrived, workers returning from the factories, people from the flats in the area and schoolchildren had already formed a crowd. We lived pretty far from the Rabook and were among the last to arrive, so we couldn't get very close. I could see they'd erected a post on a stretch of sand below the bridge. Suddenly an army Jeep drove up, followed by two or three trucks, stirring up clouds of dust. Policemen pulled a hooded man from the Jeep. Clearly weak, he could barely walk – maybe they'd tortured him before bringing him here. When they saw the traitor, everyone got excited and started shouting. They tied the man to the post. Three soldiers lined up in front of him, each with a rifle on his shoulder. There was no loudspeaker, so we couldn't understand a word of what was being said.

'What are they saying?' shouted the people standing around us.

'Can you hear anything? What did he do?'

'I think he killed a cow!'

'A cow? Who would dare do such a thing? Let him die! Serves him right!'

'Look! The soldiers are talking to him, he's trying to say something –'

Bang! Bang! Bang! The traitor had just admitted his guilt when the shots rang out. Each of the three soldiers shot him in the head, the chest and the knees. I felt no sorrow. With each shot, the man slumped a little more. There was blood everywhere. He wasn't moving. After untying him from the post, they rolled him up in some sacking. They put the body in a car, which took off immediately and disappeared from sight.

'How do you think they'll get rid of the body?' asked Jeong-ho.

'I don't know,' I answered. 'They probably take it to the mountain and dump it.'

As we watched the car drive away, it suddenly occurred to me that anyone could be executed: that it could be me. My gut seized with fear, but I stood there silent and stoic, just like the other 5,000 people around me. No one moved until we were told we could leave. The walk home was hell – it felt like the ground was collapsing under the weight of our guilty consciences. We wanted to speak, but no words would leave our mouths. It was much easier just to listen to the rhythm of our steady, robot-like footsteps. Back at home, our parents didn't speak either, even though they had just returned from the same spectacle. My mother served dinner as usual, and then we all went to bed.

We never spoke of what we had just seen.

CHAPTER SEVEN

The year I turned seventeen, my dream of attending Pyongyang University was smashed to smithereens. I should have seen it coming. Three years earlier, my sister wasn't given the research position she'd wanted. That was a bad sign. So in September 1985, when I found myself at the Chongjin University of Agriculture, it was not by choice. It was a prestigious school and the largest of the regional universities, but not at all the one I'd been aiming for. And I'd got so good at maths ... All that effort just to become a farmer!

I'd ranked third in the national university entrance exam, but clearly that wasn't enough for Pyongyang University – at least not for someone of my social rank. Two applicants from Hamgyong Province were accepted, but I was not one of them. The local authorities sent me instead to the fields, places I'd already got a taste of during those high school trips. I scrambled to find another path for myself – attending teacher's college, for example – but my requests were categorically turned down. When *Unni* was rejected, my father's anger had been tinged with suspicion; now, the doubts he had been harbouring then about the Party had been proved right: the government was ditching us. And he knew why. It was a question of *songbun* – we were cursed by my mother's bad *songbun*.

So Pyongyang University was to be no more than a dream. But what did I care for the classes on meteorology and horticulture at the Chongjin University? I had no use for learning how to plant rice and grow corn and raise animals. As if I cared about sowing seeds or breeding pigs – I already knew more than I wanted to about pigs! In fact, the only creature deserving of my attention was the dragonfly. I knew how to catch one, remove its shell and, importantly, how to eat it raw. My 'little' uncle, *Jagueun Abeoji*, had shown me how when we lived in the countryside with *Halmeoni*. At the time, he was fourteen years old and I was four. He taught me to remove the wings first without damaging the rest of the body, and then, holding the head between thumb and forefinger, you separate it from the thorax with a quick snap and finally, suck the liquid out of the abdomen. It's a technique I never forgot.

Now, like a dragonfly, it was my turn to be powerless. The State had me in the palm of its hand and was about to eat me alive. It had already ripped off my wings. My head and my body were next – it was only a matter of time.

Chongjin University (since renamed Hambook University) was one stop away from ours in Ranam, and sat opposite the Nongpo train station. Like most public buildings of the day, it was old and dusty, dating back to the time of the Japanese occupation.

To get there, we could take the *Tongguncha*, a tramway that ran three times in the morning and three times in the evening between Ranam and Nongpo. That would get us there in five minutes. The bus took fifteen. As I recall, two *ajumma* from our building worked as *Chajang*, or ticket punchers, on the bus.

But in reality, neither the trains nor the buses were really functional. They were either always late or always full – it was much better to go on foot. It was a forty-minute walk, and that's the time I needed to go over all the lessons I'd prepared the night before. The friend I walked with – not very talkative, but nice enough – would also spend the time studying. She was from Ryanggang, and her father was a senior officer in the Party. Her *songbun* was impeccable. I knew that once she earned her diploma she'd leave, and I didn't want to invest too much in a friendship with a girl I knew belonged to another world.

***

I still saw my childhood friend Hye-young. She worked in the Ammunition Factory of 10 May, named to commemorate the date of Kim Il-sung's visit. Hye-young had not passed the university entrance exam and had got a job instead. It pained me deeply to see how miserable her job made her, and how her future was all mapped out. But I was lucky: my fate was not yet completely sealed – I was holding out hope for a brighter future.

'I have a boyfriend,' she told me one day.

'Oh?'

'Yes, he works in the same factory as me. Whatever you do, don't tell my parents – they don't know about it.'

'Do you see each other often?'

'Not often, maybe once or twice a month. We take walks together in secret, far from the factory. We hold hands, we kiss, too.'

'Aren't you afraid someone will see you?'

'Yes, we are, so whenever we hear someone coming we let go of each other's hand and walk apart from each other.'

I didn't have a boyfriend, but I wasn't really tempted, either. I knew that if I did and rumours started circulating, weekly self-criticism sessions weren't far behind. Anyway, all the boys my age were off doing their military service. And the university was hardly a place to meet people: we all had so much work to do there was no time to fall in love.

***

Classes were deadly dull. One day I defied the head of the class. He was one of the guys who began his military service right out of high school and didn't finish for another ten years. These guys were almost thirty when they got to university – they had trouble studying again after such a long break from it.

We called him *Dongmu*, or comrade. He was from Kangwon Province. He stood at 1.6 metres tall, or 5 foot 3, and he terrorised our class, making us do not only our own homework but that of all the students who had just finished their military service. At first, I simply refused – I had enough to do without doing other people's school work. He punished me by making me clean the classroom during the lunch break and after school. After a month of that I gave in and started doing the extra homework without complaining – I didn't want the 'anti-regime' symbol placed next to my name on the call list.

During my second year at university, I won first place in a maths contest. That gave me the equivalent of a degree in maths, and that's what allowed me to avoid becoming a farmer. 'How many soldiers are still living, if among the ten American soldiers, six are killed?' We were always on the battlefield with those poor Americans, but clearly it was a teaching method that worked well.

***

During the second year of my studies, in April 1987, I was sent off to do six months of military training. To my dismay, it turned out that at university it was not enough to do your studies, you also had to learn to make war. In high school, we had spent at most a week at camp learning to handle a gun. At university, we were preparing to do battle with America: a war might break out at any moment, and we had to be ready.

Our first training session took place at Camp Kangduk in Songpyong, near the city of Ranam, where female artillery troops were based. These women had chosen a career in the military, and knew how to fire anti-aircraft cannons. We wore the same uniforms as they did and trained outside all day under a blazing sun that burned our faces. We were nineteen-year-old soldiers with guns that were far too heavy for us.

So this is the army, I thought.

Between our sweat and our periods, with access to neither showers nor hygienic napkins, the dormitories stank. There were twelve of us per room. To have any hope of sleeping at night, we had to leave the windows open all day or we'd suffocate from the acrid stench given off by the blankets that were blackened with filth and had probably never been washed. How were we supposed to live in such conditions? Why had these women chosen the army over other careers? Was it possible that they saw this horrible place as an escape? How could that be? Wasn't being an *ajumma* better than this? These questions remained unanswered until much later, when the fate of one horrendous woman played out before my eyes like a grotesque carnival: that woman was my mother.

It was also during my second year of university that I spent fifty days in Chongsong, a city in Onsung, as a volunteer helping with rural development. When I told my parents I was going to do this, they begged me to be on my guard day and night, never to go out alone. We would be near coal mines, they said, and the prisoners who worked in them were extremely dangerous. 'Coal mine', in fact, was another name for *Suyongso*, or prison camp.

To get to there, I had to take the train to Hoeryong, the birthplace of Kim Il-sung's first wife, then transfer to a steam train and ride that for an hour. Based on what my father had told me, I expected to see prisoners everywhere, as he had described – shaved heads and dark grey uniforms. But as I walked out of the station an entirely different tableau unfolded before my eyes.

It was like a scene from one of those black-and-white documentary films I'd seen in school about the Japanese occupation. Men walked the streets tied together at the waist by rope. There were dirty children, too, their necks covered in sores, the skin on their hands cracked, eyes as weary-looking as the eyes of old men. It was raining, and you could hear the *flip flop, flip flop* of the black rubber shoes, or *gomusin*, in the streets. I had never seen such misery. When I finally made it to the place we were staying, I found twenty women packed into a single room. The roof was full of leaks, and this was the only dry room. This was where I would sleep for the next fifty nights, with these twenty young women who had just finished their studies and been called to 'modernise the countryside'.

This would be me in four years …

Chongsong was one of those cities without a soul, built by the army and construction crews as part of the rural development effort. The young women laboured non-stop in the fields, far more efficiently than me. I'd always believed myself to be a fast worker, but next to these women I was a tortoise. My fingers turned yellow from picking tobacco leaves and my skin went raw from planting corn and beans all day. Far from leading the pack as I had before, I would barely finish planting my seed lot by the end of the day. An insidious fear of failure came to inhabit me. My spiritual fatigue was equal to my physical exhaustion, and both were unbearable. By the end, I had lost weight, my skin was rough and sunburnt, and every step I took caused a searing pain.

Unni had told me this was going to be hard, I reminded myself. *She made it. There's no reason I won't too.*

***

When I returned home from Chongsong, a huge surprise was waiting: we had a television set! It was black and white, Russian made, with a much bigger screen than televisions made in Korea.

'Now you don't have to go to Mrs Jang's to watch telly, you can do it in the comfort of your own home,' my father said with a radiant smile as he dusted the screen with a dry cloth. 'There are only ten of these in the whole building!' he added excitedly.

'My business is doing a little better,' my mother offered, as though to justify the sudden arrival of the TV set.

'Speaking of which, *Myeongsil umma*, you should take a break. You've worked enough, you can rest now,' my father said, gazing benevolently at my mother.

In Korea, spouses call each other not by their given names but by the phrase 'mother of' or 'father of' followed by the name of the eldest boy or, if there's no boy, the name of the eldest girl. That was common custom. What was less common was for the mother to go away as often as mine did to do her business ...

CHAPTER SEVEN

My mother was a born entrepreneur. She had traded the pigs for the television set – a stroke of genius. No one else had yet had the idea of selling pigs and using the profits to start another business. She bought Chinese products in cities near the border and sold them in little local markets. This was the beginning of the *Jangmadang*, or black markets, which would soon become the only means of survival for the country's *ajumma*. Under a bridge, in the outlying parts of a city, the improvised markets consisted of merchandise spread on the ground. Squatting on their heels in the traditional Korean waiting position, the merchant women would jump up whenever a police officer appeared. They sold and traded all sorts of things – food, crockery, clothing, shoes, comic books, hardware. I remember one day when our mother brought us back some clothes from China made of quality cloth. This was such a change from the itchy acrylic we were used to. They were pink, yellow, sky blue – bright colours we rarely saw in North Korea. I don't know why, but I can still picture one of my mother's purchases, a vermilion-red blanket with a green parrot in the middle.

***

In February 1988, after two nights and three days of arduous walking, I arrived at the birthplace of King Jong-il on Mount Paektu. One of three students chosen to represent Chongjin University, I was proud to take part in the excursion.

Located in the North, near the border with China, Mount Paektu is the highest peak on the Korean Peninsula. Our textbooks told us that Kim Jong-Il was born on 16 February 1942 during the war against Japan. His father, Kim Il-sung, led his army from this mountaintop. Thinking about it now, it occurs to me that other sources, such as Soviet archives, tell us something different: that he was born Yuri Irsenovich Kim, in Vyatskoye, Khabarovsk Krai, in Russia, in 1941 – a year earlier than we were taught!

I lost myself in the magic of the dense forest that covered the mountainside. Inscriptions that had been carved into certain trees by the Kim family lent an air of solemnity to the place, a sense of profound historic significance. The fact that Mount Paektu is an active volcano (though inactive that day) added to the drama of the place. The sun shone on Heaven Lake in the caldera, ringed with treeless rocky peaks dusted with snow. This was my sun, the sun that opened my eyes to the beauty of morning's first light, the twinkling of stars, the blue of the sky. This was the sun which comforted me, listened to me in silence, and yet, this was the sun which dazzled me at times to the point of blindness.

***

When my sister *Unni* finished her studies in June 1988, a friend of hers introduced her to Hong Sang-cheol, a good-looking boy with smooth, jet-black hair. He was only a little older than she was. One day he showed up at our house and asked to see her. I took an instant dislike to him, and told him she was out and that he should go. My brother Jeong-ho had the same reaction and congratulated me for sending him away. Meanwhile, *Unni* had no use for our 'gut feelings' and continued to see him in secret. They met in Sunam-guyok, a district on the far side of Chongjin. That was where Sang-cheol, a fisherman, lived with his family.

And what a poor family it was. Five brothers and sisters, and bad *songbun* to boot – the worst.

'Out of the question!' my father shouted when she returned from one of their trysts. 'You are not marrying him. He didn't even do his military service. He's a shady fellow!'

'Abeoji,' Unni said calmly, 'you are the eldest in your family, like I am. You too know what it's like to spend your life being scrutinised by your family, to have to lead a "model" life. I don't want to live with this pressure.'

I can't believe it, I thought to myself as I hid behind the kitchen door, *she's talking back to* Abeoji. *She who never said a word for so long … I'm so glad I'm the youngest daughter!*

'I've found you someone much better than that illiterate fisherman!' my uncle declared another day. 'He works in the army and has impeccable *songbun*. What do you say?' he asked, trying to sound playful. He sensed there was tension in the air.

'No, thank you,' my sister said firmly. 'I'm not interested.'

She left the kitchen.

This was a bombshell. I'd put *Unni* on a pedestal all her life, yet here she was, acting out. Such an independent spirit she had, and such courage! I was beside myself with admiration.

My mother was the only one who was not against the marriage. She probably thought there was a lot of money to be made selling fish on the black market – her latest money-making scheme – or at least enough to feed a family. Finding enough to eat had become a real problem. My father was thinking about the long term, about his descendants. His grandchildren's future would be ruined by his son-in-law's bad *songbun* – and he was all too familiar with that particular pain. My mother, on the other hand, could think only of the present and cared about concrete things – like being able to put a bowl of rice on the table.

***

That semester, our biology classes were held outside, on a hill near the Soosung bus station. Ten minutes from there was a prison called Chongjin Soosung *Kyowhaso*, or Camp 25. I'd never heard of it before. The high walls were topped with electric barbed wire, as were the four guard towers rising up in each of the four corners of the courtyard. It was a terrifying place. The immediate surroundings were off limits, but the hillside wasn't. From here I could look directly into the open courtyard. There I saw prisoners who were making bicycles and others who were tilling the earth. All of them had shaved heads and wore dark-grey uniforms. From where I sat I couldn't see if they were wearing shoes or not. Near the heavy metal entrance gate sat the trucks that carried the prisoners away in the morning and brought them back at the end of the day. When the prisoners returned through the gate their heads were bowed, just as they were when they left. But was I seeing clearly? Could it be that there were old people among them, all hunched over? And were those women, and children too? Could they have ended up there because of the famous guilt by association, or *Yeonjwaje*?

The six months we spent doing experiments on the hill and the fact that I could not tell anyone what I'd seen plunged me into a state of anxiety. I had to manage the two Jihyun living inside me – the one who believed in *Juche* down to her bones, and the one who had just been wrenched from her childhood dreams. I often went about wearing a mask of white cotton, which had strings that hooked behind my ears and which covered my nose and mouth. It protected me from the outside world, but also enabled me to hide something that was eating away at my insides, something that terrified me: behind the iron curtain was a world I knew nothing about.

From time to time we heard gunshots. People said it meant someone had tried to escape. Whenever that happened I would tell my mother about it, hoping she would reassure me. But she only ever answered with an indifferent 'Yes, I know' as she chopped kimchi in the kitchen. Prisoners were dying every day – being shot at was not enough to discourage them from trying to escape.

What had these poor families done that was so terrible that they were condemned by the National Security police, or *Bowibu*, whose single accusation cast a net over all the members of a family, even distant relatives? What was so criminal that the *Bowibu* had to get involved? Thirty years later, I still don't know.

***

One spring evening in 1989, we were awakened at 10pm by shouting and screaming at the far end of the hall. Police were pounding on the door of flat 1. The father of the family who lived there was off visiting his parents in the country. At home were the mother, who worked in a pharmaceutical plant, a twenty-year-old son named Nam-goon and two girls – one fourteen, the other ten. I knew Nam-goon pretty well. He was doing his military service. I'd run into him in the hallway a few days earlier, and he'd told me he was home on three days' leave.

Everything happened fast. Through the open doorway I could see Nam-goon's face. He looked devastated. Doubtless he had just learned the real reason the army had allowed him to come home. Before he had a chance to speak, the two secret agents ripped off the uniform he was wearing and ordered him to change into a T-shirt and trousers. They then handcuffed him, his mother and his sisters and led the family away. I didn't know exactly where they were going, but I had some idea of the fate that awaited them.

The next morning, I heard Mrs Choi, the building manager, talking in the corridor. I cracked open the door of our flat and listened. A group of *ajumma* had gathered around her.

'The agents took their blankets and plates, but I'm going to see what's left,' she said as she entered the empty flat. 'Mrs Kim, come with me.'

A few minutes later, Mrs Choi and Mrs Kim emerged with a wad of banknotes in their hands.

'100 won! This must be the money she was saving up to give her daughters a nice wedding,' said the building manager.

It was the equivalent of a month's salary!

'Oh yeah? How does she manage to put so much money aside? We barely have enough to buy food,' said one of the *ajumma*.

'Actually, saving money isn't bad enough to land your family in a prison camp. Spending some time in a correction centre would've done the job. There must be something else going on …'

'What else has she got up to? That secretive little …'

'It's not about her, it's about her husband. He's a landowner. They've been keeping an eye on him for a while now. A few days ago, he drank too much and criticised the Party, blaming it for how poor he is. They arrested him yesterday while he was at his parents' in the country. Criticising the State, now *that's* a serious crime. That's why they arrested the whole family. Guilty by association – you know, *Yeonjwaje*.'

We never found out what became of the 100 won.

'Birds listen in the daytime, mice listen at night.' That night, the proverb took on new meaning. *Be careful*, I told myself over and over as I quietly closed the door to the flat. *The State is God. It would be so forever and ever*. Hiding under my blankets, I began to cry. I'd grown up with the Nams. They were a happy family. One beer, a few misplaced words, and five lives were ruined. It wasn't sadness so much as fear that I felt for that family in flat number 1. It was the same fear that had gripped me on the hillside in Soosung.

Flat number 1 remained empty for a year.

***

In July 1989, it was our turn to receive a visit from the *Bowibu*.

The day they knocked on our door, my mother was the only one home. Later, when we got home from school, she was still emotional. Breathlessly, she told us what had happened. She said they told her that they were there to announce the arrival of someone who had come to North Korea to take part in the thirteenth International Festival of Youth and Students.

'Really?' she'd said, surprised. 'But doesn't the festival take place in Pyongyang every year?'

The officer told our mother that this year it was Chongjin's turn to hold the festival, and that our family had been chosen as a host family, thanks to a distant uncle who had recently been named a member of the Party. At the end of the visit Mum walked the officers all the way down the corridor. She was so overjoyed by the news that she was still bowing and saying *Kamsahamnida* (thank you) even after they had disappeared from sight.

'This will be good for my *songbun*!' she cried, ecstatic. 'But I'll admit I nearly died of fright when I realised someone from the *Bowibu* was at the door.'

What we later learned was that the story about the distant uncle who'd joined the Party was merely a fabrication used to justify their coming to our flat. It was a 'courtesy visit', if you will, to the family of a deserter. Our mother in fact had a thousand reasons to be afraid of the visit from the *Bowibu* that day.

From time to time, I'd try to imagine this grandfather-deserter. *Our Nation and Its People*, a documentary I watched on television, gave me a little hope. The show was about deserters who had come back to visit North Korea out of a sense of nostalgia. Maybe our grandfather would visit one day, too, I thought. Maybe he would bring gifts. New clothes. Maybe he missed us terribly. What kind of man was he? I wondered. Did he ever think about the daughter he'd left behind? A visa for North Korea was expensive. The people in the film must have been rich to be able to come back. And my grandfather? How might he have made his fortune? The South was so poor. Never mind. All that mattered to me was that if he came back I would be able to go to university wearing new clothes.

New clothes, like the ones my uncle *Jagueun Abeoji* and his wife had worn on their wedding day. Now they had two daughters – one four years old and the other, Yeong-wha, a baby of eleven months – and they were expecting twins. The night before Yeong-wha's birthday, my uncle's wife started having contractions. My uncle brought her to the hospital but things went very badly: the twins did not live, and my aunt never woke from the pain pills an incompetent midwife had given her. As if the death of his wife and twins were not painful enough, *Jagueun Abeoji* was not able to honour them with a decent burial, and that devastated him. His wife had died not at home but in hospital, and that was bad luck. Having a funeral might bring a curse upon him. My parents decided to let Yeong-wha live with us until her father was better. The elder daughter stayed with him. He lived a fifty-minute walk from us, near the farm where he worked. We visited him as often as possible.

Yeong-wha didn't understand why she couldn't see her mum. She wept and wailed every night. I would bring her close to me under the covers and tell her that her mum was coming soon to get her but that she had to sleep and eat well so she would be in good shape when she came.

A year later, Yeong-wha returned to a home without a mother.

CHAPTER EIGHT

Jihyun has been invited to attend the Asian Women of Achievement awards ceremony. In her application, which she'd submitted a few months earlier, she wrote of her commitment to raise awareness about the situation in North Korea. Her expectations weren't high but she was glad to have done it, and she was thrilled to have been invited to the event.

I'm so excited I send her an SMS:

'Any news?'

It's late. My kids are in bed, the table's set for breakfast and the front door is locked. Standing at the bottom of the staircase, I'm about to set the alarm and go upstairs when the screen of my mobile phone lights up, catching my eye:

'Bit disappointed, didn't receive Social and Humanitarian award.'

That's a pity. But Jihyun is so strong, she won't be devastated. This is nothing compared to what she's already lived through. Yet this is the first time I've ever heard her express disappointment, and my heart breaks a little. What should I say to her? How can I console her? She was so deserving of that award …

'So sorry, Jihyun, but it was such a great honour just to have been one of the finalists.'

'True. You're right. Thank you.'

I'm still standing there at the foot of the stairs, mobile in hand. Should I send her a long note to comfort her? Call her right away to talk, or simply go to bed for now and plan to call her tomorrow? Finally, I make up my mind: I'll send her a brief 'Good night, talk to you tomorrow.' But just as I'm about to start typing, I see the number 3 next to Jihyun's name. Three text messages? What's happened in the past few moments?

'My name's been called.'

'Chairman's Award?'

'About to receive Chairman's Award. They're calling me to the podium. Will phone you later.'

My throat tightens. I muffle my cry of joy because it's twenty-two minutes past midnight and everyone's asleep. My head is spinning because I have to keep silent, but my heart is bursting with happiness. This is about more than just winning an award, it's about more than trophies and speeches and photographs. It's about *being recognised for eight years of relentless work*. That's why my heart is pounding so. What a stupendous moment, a real sign of hope. And what an accomplishment – the 2018 Asian Women of Achievement Award!

AWA has been honouring female victims of violence who denounce crimes against humanity since 1999. Today, 10 May 2018, Jihyun has received the Chairman's Award in recognition of her optimism, her ability to inspire and serve as a model for the next generation and her drive to change the world.

***

A few days later I meet Jihyun at Heathrow Airport. She's to be the guest of honour at a conference on human rights in Geneva and I'm going with her. We rarely get violent storms in London, but today the airport is on high alert. The flight schedule won't be posted for another hour. I look at the sky. Perfect – we'll have plenty of time for her to tell me all about the AWA awards ceremony.

In the departures lounge, we are merely two passengers among thousands. This anonymity is oddly reassuring: it creates a space in which we feel safe sharing confidences.

Jihyun tells me that during the AWA awards ceremony everything became clear to her. Suddenly she understood why for so many years she had been driven to fight for something greater than her own life.

She could easily have settled for raising her three children in Manchester without ever telling her story, but she didn't – she spoke out. 'Now, other refugees must do the same. I want to believe I've given them hope,' she says with emotion. That resonates for me. Whenever a political reality rears its head, my identity as a Korean is roused. Am I not one of those very women who has settled for a little life of raising children? What else do I actually *do* besides listen to her?

I listen to you, Jihyun. And listening is more than just hearing, it's taking in information. It's paying attention. It's decoding reality. And what do I do when I stop listening? I speak out through my writing. My pen brings you to life, it allows you to blossom, it turns you back into that lively and talkative girl who was so full of joie de vivre, that girl who was suppressed for so long. I in turn am amazed by you, by all you've managed to accomplish, and I no longer try to hide the blissful delight I feel towards life. As you know, I grew up speaking Korean, English and Spanish, but my 'real' language is French – it's the language of my writing, the language that transforms our conversation into something others can experience. It's the language that suits our Korean soul so well and allows us to create something in our very own way. Thank you for giving me permission to write in this language.

'When you arrived in England eight years ago, you didn't even speak English. You didn't socialise. Look how far you've come,' I tell Jihyun proudly.

I think back to that period of loneliness that she's told me about. North Korea and China were behind her, but instead of feeling safe in Manchester, England, day and night she was overcome by fits of despair at the thought of the parents and siblings she'd left behind.

How did she make it through that time?

Two years. That's how long I've wanted to ask her this question, but I've never dared. I don't want to offend her or rush her, I want to handle her feelings with care. I don't want to undermine the delicate balance we've managed to achieve in our relationship, this friendship undergirded by a deep sense of female solidarity. I keep myself from talking about how people seek help in the West. I want to tell her about 'therapy' but I don't even know how to say it in Korean. Then I realise the word doesn't even exist – for the obvious reason that it's a Western concept. I can't apply a plaster before healing the wound.

'How did you manage?' I ask her at last, a bit shyly.

'The British government offered me aid. I didn't know what kind of aid, though, so I said no. I didn't believe it would help. I didn't see how people who hadn't been through what I'd been through could possibly help me.'

'I understand that.'

'I never left home. I kept all my pain to myself – I didn't share it with anyone, including my husband, even though he's North Korean and knows my situation better than anyone.'

'He wouldn't have understood that you were suffering?'

'Oh yes, he would have. It's not that. It's just – how can you talk about sexual assault with your husband?'

Outside the large glass window separating us from the tarmac, we can see the grey sky, heavy with clouds that are ready to burst. Wrapped in our raincoats, we remain silent. The swathe of cinder-coloured clouds swells and fills the heavens as though cursing us. I'm hoping with all my heart that the airline representative will make an announcement to release us from this spell.

'You know, I can tell you lots of things because you're a woman,' Jihyun says.

I look at her.

'For example, I couldn't talk to a man about how girls in North Korea handle being on their period. Do you know what they do?'

'I know there aren't sanitary napkins,' I stammer. 'I think you mentioned that in one of our conversations.'

'The napkins are made of *gajae*.'

'Gajae? Gauze? You mean like we use for compresses? I can't hide my shock.'

'Yes, that's all there is. You have to wash it by hand after every use. Sometimes there's not even soap. "Sanitary" napkin. As if! At home, sometimes we would boil them to disinfect them. My mother forbade us to dry them out in the open because it was indecent to let a man see them – you had to do it out of sight.'

Life there is so challenging for women …

I think about South Korean women, for whom cultivating their beautiful skin has become a national sport – even more important than helping a neighbour in distress – and suddenly I feel racked with guilt. Seoul has become a mecca for plastic surgery. It's the city with the highest volume of beauty products sold per square metre in the world. Indeed, the number-one concern of the 'beauties of Kangnam' is the famous Korean five-step beauty ritual: serum, moisturiser, sunscreen, base and finally the BB cream, for a flawless complexion before applying make-up. One way to avoid facing reality is to lose yourself under layers of face cream.

'Do you think you've suffered more because you're a woman?' I ask, already annoyed by the absurdity of my earlier observation. 'I'm thinking about your poor aunt, the one who died in childbirth at the hospital. Is it safer to give birth at home?'

'Oh, much safer. Want to know how my sister gave birth at the hospital? They told her to stand on her bed and jump off, over and over, to make the baby drop! *That's* what it's like to give birth in the hospital.'

'Oh my God …'

What you're telling me makes no sense, Jihyun. It's absurd how different our lives have been. I don't know whether to laugh or cry. Yet it's all so real.

'You have no idea. The whole world has no idea. Life there is unimaginable, and no one has the right to complain.'

You're exactly right. It was unimaginable – until the day I met you. Do you know what I told myself two years ago, after we did that interview with Amnesty International at your place in Manchester? I told myself I never wanted to see you again. I'd only accepted the job to help out my friend. It was a fluke that I ended up there with you. After the interview, the weight of everything you shared, your pain, your personal story in all its intimacy – well, it was too much. I couldn't deal with it. I wanted to forget everything, to go back to my safe, comfortable life in London and focus on my usual trivial concerns. With time, I've grown ashamed of my cowardice. With time, I've learned to make peace with my weaknesses by linking your story to mine. With time, I've seen that it's possible not to give in to day-to-day mediocrity, and I've started to change the way I think about life. You awakened in me something that must have been programmed from the start – a voice that had been muted and that wanted only to be heard.

The sight of a thirty-something Asian man in a black raincoat brings me back to the present. He's watching us from a distance. I noticed him in the crowd when we were looking at the departures board. At the time I didn't pay him any attention, but now he is more conspicuous. I turn back to Jihyun while keeping him in my field of vision. I'm about to speak again when she says, 'Do you see that man in the black raincoat? He's been watching us for a while now.'

'He has?' I say as if nothing's amiss.

So you noticed him, too, Jihyun. You are so perceptive. Don't worry, I understand the risks you're running and I'm on my guard. I can't tell you this, but I always have to be on high alert when we're together.

'We have to be careful. You never know. Remember what happened to Kim Jong-un's half-brother in the Kuala Lumpur Airport? Things happen in a flash.'

Anxiety rises in me. I sit up straighter in my chair. I take a few seconds to think but I don't know what to say. Admitting that I'm afraid will only unleash a whole cascade of worries. I have to come up with something, so I say, 'That poor guy can watch us all he wants. You know how Asians in a crowd always look at each other, wondering if they're Korean or Japanese or Chinese. Don't you ever do that? I do! That's all he's up to. Don't worry.'

I hand Jihyun the packet of biscuits I've brought for the trip, take her by the shoulders and turn her to face me so her back is to the man. She's smiling again. Nervous as I am relieved, I gather my wits and pick up where we left off.

'We were talking about the status of women in North Korea. I was wondering, for example, does divorce exist?'

'Far from it! Unless the husband is a deserter, like my maternal grandfather, divorce is not an option. I remember a woman in my neighbourhood. I thought she was a widow. She was raising two kids alone. One day her husband came back – he had just spent ten years in prison. The entire time he was gone she had tried to begin divorce proceedings but had never succeeded. She had to spend the rest of her life with a convict, she had no choice. Can you imagine?'

'I won't ask if homosexuality is accepted, then.'

'I didn't even know what the word meant until I arrived in England. When I was filling out my application for a British passport, I ticked the "same sex marriage" box because I thought it meant you were married to someone of the same ethnic group.'

At first, I'm so surprised I say nothing.

Then we both start laughing so hard we can't stop, giggling like two schoolgirls who have just learned a naughty word. Just as a spider delicately spins her web, the threads of our friendship are reaching out and entwining us, weaving us together ever more tightly. *It's because we're laughing*, I think to myself. *It's laughter that's creating our bond*. My thoughts turn again to that strange country where all laughter is fake, where everyone is pretending just to stay alive, where people are starving but act as if they have everything they need, where the only tears allowed are those that are shed for the Great Leader. No surprise, then, that there's never an uprising, that the people never revolt. Apart from family ties – and even those are being destroyed – nothing unites them. There's nothing to create a bond among them and create a sense of solidarity with each other. Misery alone is not enough to bring human beings together – they need happiness, too.

Jihyun is watching the clouds move across the sky. Her expression is mild, peaceful. I resume our conversation.

'As we were saying, you didn't talk about anything with your husband or anyone else …'

'In the end, I agreed to talk to a group of women from Panos London.'

'Panos? Never heard of them.'

'It's a charity that gives a voice to people in distress. They rang me up one day and asked if I would tell them about my experience. The first time I spoke of it was with them. It felt good to be talking to women, they understood me. I didn't feel alone any more. It was as though the group's energy shook me out of my funk. Speaking of which, I don't think it's pure coincidence that two women are writing this book: we not only speak the same language and share a Korean identity, but we share our identity as women, too.'

I think about that for a moment.

It's true, we are writing from the perspective of women who grew up under Confucianism, the patriarchal system that shaped our childhood and adolescence. We espoused and internalised it in spite of ourselves. I try to articulate how it plays out in us. I know that despite men's traditional role in Confucianism, both our fathers – Jihyun's as much as mine – managed to make their girls' education a priority. They helped us become strong, confident women within a clearly defined belief system based on filial piety, education, integrity, compassion and respect for others. The Confucian worldview is far from perfect, but at least it enables us to maintain faith in our roots. Rather than waiting for the rest of the world to solve our problems, wouldn't drawing on the strengths of our own country – the country that unites us – give us hope for reconciliation?

I come back to the conversation.

'You know, when you speak to me in Korean, you convey to me a certain feeling – it's your choice of words, but it's also something between and beyond your words. Your voice is full of … I believe it's what we call *Han* in Korean, a melancholy of the soul. The shared heritage of national identity and the trauma of separation. When you're amazed by something you're telling me and you end your sentence with *tcham!* [Really!] or *guiga makhyeo!* [It takes my breath away!], it's like … it's like it's you and me against the world. I'm no longer in London, I'm in Korea with you. As though our fatherland were being reinvented out of words rather than land. As though language were all we needed to coexist. During the Japanese occupation, from 1910 until 1945, when Korean was forbidden and Korean surnames were replaced with Japanese-sounding ones, we lost our identity. A whole part of human history, erased. Forgotten.'

'Your description of *Han* explains so well why I wanted a Korean to write this book – precisely to express these kinds of unspoken meanings. They're complicated and difficult to explain.'

When I start a sentence, you finish it. When you disagree with me, you wait politely for me to finish my argument before saying, with your kind and generous spirit, 'It makes sense that you don't understand this point, it's because you haven't lived in North Korea.' You're no longer entirely North Korean and I'm no longer entirely South Korean. We've become simply Korean. Two Korean women. Our shared suffering – the pain of our divided country – is enough to unite us.

'At the end of the day,' I say with some wonder, 'you and I lived through neither the Japanese occupation nor the Korean War. So why are we both so inhabited by this sense of an oppressed culture?'

Jihyun looks down as though she's about to bring up a painful memory.

'When an event is ongoing, it's impossible to mourn it. I'm thinking about having to abandon my dying father when I fled. Grief sets in and stays with you for life. I have never been able to mourn my father. The same goes for our country – the division of Korea into two countries is ongoing, so we cannot mourn it, and that is why we suffer so.'

Jihyun raises her eyes to look at me. There's nothing more to be said. She's explained our national history, our personal history, us – how we're weighed down by silence, by something not yet expressed, by an absence of words that has afflicted several generations. *Han* is the burden of a reality both emotional and historic.

'Attention! All passengers travelling to Geneva, please proceed to gate number fifteen.'

But I only half-hear the announcement. I look around for the man in the black raincoat: he's nowhere to be seen. I was right to pretend not to notice him. What was he doing there if he wasn't on our flight? We'll probably never know. No matter. I give myself over to thoughts of *Han*. It's as though our conversation has validated my feelings. I reach down deep inside myself and find new strength. My whole body crackles with this new sensation as I walk towards … which gate was it now?

CHAPTER NINE

The nineties was one of the worst decades North Korea had ever known. Diesel for cooking stoves ran out. Oil lamps replaced electric light bulbs. Instead of running water, we were forced to draw buckets from the river. And supplies in the distribution centres were running thin – people could only count on the black market for food now. In 1991, the press blamed the meagre harvests on flooding and drought while utterly failing to mention the collapse of the Soviet Union, a country on which North Korea had become highly dependent for crop production. This was the beginning of a famine the State dubbed *Gonan Eui Haeng-goon*, or The March of Suffering. A gruelling ordeal that would drag on for ten years, the true extent of it would become known only in the years that followed. Officially it didn't begin until 1994 but in fact, by 1991, it was already a reality.

This was also the year of my father's heart attack. Because he couldn't work at his factory job for several months, our family could not count on his salary to provide for us. Fortunately, Mum's business was flourishing, so we were spared the fate of becoming homeless. The trains no longer worked due to the blackout, but *Eomeoni* still made it to Musan, a city on the border with China, to sell her dried seafood. With her gift for negotiation, she would bribe drivers with alcohol, cigarettes and cash to let her hide in the open bed of their lorries, even though they were designed to carry merchandise, not people.

My mother would be gone for weeks at a time. She would buy octopus and sea cucumber on the north-east coast, dry it and then sell it at the market in Musan. She would then outfit her stall in the

Sunam-guyok and Ban-jug markets, near where we lived, with electrical items, shoes and clothing. One day she came home with a radio – a rare, expensive object. We used it to listen to songs about Kim Il-sung. There was only one radio station, but listening to music was a great luxury. To this day, I can remember a piece played by the Pochonbo Orchestra. It had been written in celebration of the defeat of Japanese troops in a battle that took place on 4 July 1937. My favourite music group was the Wangjaesan Light Music Band, formed after the battle of Wangjae in Onsung in 1933. The purpose of the group was to mark the date when Kim Il-sung had called a meeting to re-energise anti-Japanese activities in occupied Korea. While my father opposed my mother's black-market activities, he had to admit that if we were dressed in handsome Chinese-made clothes and had corn and potatoes to ease our hunger, it was thanks to her.

By 1991, my brother, Jeong-ho, had turned into a handsome fifteen-year-old. He wore a black suit with a detachable white collar that he washed himself every evening, as well as white trainers, also made in China. Svelte and elegant, he cared a lot about his appearance. I still remember that he even sewed on his own buttons using our mother's sewing machine. Not only was Jeong-ho physically attractive, but he was also a hard-working student and extremely good at football, and eventually he became captain of the Regional Football League. He often invited his best friend, Park Sung-jin, home and we had some great times together. Among my brother's classmates there were also the less studious ones who indulged in the pleasures of tobacco, sometimes even marijuana. Cannabis plants lined the roads of Chongjin, but we had no idea that their leaves and twigs were used to make pot. We diligently gathered the seeds that had fallen on the ground and handed them over to the government, just as we'd gathered silkworms in the eighties. In smoking pot, my brother and his friends didn't even know they were doing drugs. To them, it was just another kind of cigarette.

***

CHAPTER NINE

In September 1991, when I was twenty-three years old, I started teaching maths at Saegori-dong High School in the northern part of Chongjin. Despite the bleak mood that hung over the country, I loved my job. It was thanks to my mother that I'd landed the position. Once again, she had managed to cleverly use corruption to her advantage, bribing the officials in the work-placement office at Chongjin University with Chinese cigarettes and dried octopus. Thanks to her, I escaped becoming a farmer – the logical outcome for a graduate with a degree in Agriculture and Meteorology. For that, I was infinitely grateful.

Every morning at 7am I was greeted by these words above the school entrance:

BAE-OU-JA, BAE-OU-JA, GUEURIGO TTO BAE-OU JA!

LONG LIVE EDUCATION, LONG LIVE EDUCATION! INDEED, LONG LIVE EDUCATION!

In 1980, aged twelve, I had entered the gates of this high school in Nam-Chongjin, my heart fluttering with anticipation at the thought of meeting my new teacher. Eleven years later, at twenty-three, that teacher was *me*.

I had about forty twelve-year-old pupils. This would be my class for the next six years until they finished their secondary schooling. My favourite was Park Young-mi. Far from being the best pupil, she nevertheless always wore a smile and worked hard at her studies. I saw a good deal of her because she lived in my neighbourhood. During one of our walks together, she shared that she was the youngest of four girls and that her father had volunteered to fight in Libya in order to feed his family.

I earned between 10 and 20 won per hour, cash – less than one hundredth of a euro today. It wasn't much, but that was the salary of a novice teacher and I told myself that as soon as I got a promotion I would get a raise. I stayed at school until 8 or 9pm every night, preparing my classes for the next day and then spending the rest of the evening studying for the exams that would enable me to land a promotion. I'd thought I'd put exams behind me once I left university, but the world of teaching was highly political and hierarchical: if I was going to make it, I needed to figure out fast how things worked.

***

Barely a year had gone by since I'd started teaching when I began to notice changes in my pupils. They no longer smiled, they came to school hungry; they would lay their heads on their desks, too weary to write, much less focus on their lessons. I began to feel useless. To think that when I was their age, seated on the other side of the podium, I had been full of hope, with confidence in the future and the will to please both my teacher and the State.

One day in February 1992, *Eunjoo umma*, the delegate for our block of flats, put up a poster in the entryway.

'It's a poem written by Kim Il-sung marking the fifty-second birthday of his son, Kim Jong-Il,' she told me when I came home from school. 'You must learn it by heart.'

Because of her role, *Eunjoo umma* was obliged to come off as a strict authoritarian, but in reality she was a sweet, gentle woman who lived on the second storey with her two children. In 1990, when my family moved to this newly built block, the Port of Chongjin Flats, she had shown us a particularly warm welcome.

'I do?' I said weakly, exhausted after the long day.

'Yes, you do! Everyone must memorise it, no exceptions!'

I was starving, drunk with fatigue, still in shock over the sight of so many people begging in the street. And now I was being asked to memorise a poem about the 'two lives' – one earthly, the other political. The body that over time dies while the 'political soul' lives on … As the phrases echoed in my head, the pale faces of my pupils flashed before my eyes. It was as though a swirling wind had just blown away twenty years' worth of dust. I saw myself slip into the skin of a new me as I grasped the truth.

CHAPTER NINE

We must nourish the 'political soul' if we are to be saved? But what about our bodies? Who will feed us? No amount of political 'food' would keep me alive. Nothing could replace a bowl of rice, not even a poem by Kim Il-sung!

***

In 1993, when I was twenty-five, all rationing ceased. 'Come back tomorrow! We haven't had a delivery today!' the workers would say as my mother and I lingered at the Public Distribution Centre. Without daring to complain, and with no hard feelings, we'd return the next day, and the next, only to find the Centre as empty as ever.

'Is it just our neighbourhood, or is it like this everywhere?' an *ajumma* asked one day at the Centre. 'I don't get it. Why aren't you getting any more deliveries?'

'I don't know any more than you,' replied a worker from across the counter. 'I hear the South Koreans sent us poisoned fertiliser and all our rice paddies have been ruined.'

That poor man was only repeating what he'd been told. It wasn't just our neighbourhood. I'd suspected as much: the food shortage had hit the entire country and the government had launched a 'two meals a day instead of three' campaign, citing the example of the Great Leader Kim Il-sung who, as he fought against the Japanese in 1945, proclaimed: 'We must know hunger!' Yet he didn't hesitate to take the bowls of rice from the hands of the people in order to feed the soldiers who were defending the nation – apparently it was our duty to help feed the army.

Hunger inhabited my classroom. I watched as all my pupils rapidly lost weight, but it was Park Young-mi's weakened state that was by far the most alarming. She had just turned thirteen. Her grades began to plummet. One day in April, she didn't attend class. In general, my pupils missed school for one of two reasons: either they were roaming the streets looking for ways to alleviate their gnawing hunger, or they were so malnourished that they could no longer make the trek to school. I decided to go see Young-mi after school. When I arrived at her apartment, her family greeted me flatly, silently, as though there were no words for the scene before us. Young-mi lay on a mattress on the floor, her eyes closed and her stomach as swollen as a pregnant woman's. I'd never seen such a distended belly on a child and I didn't know then that it signalled the beginning of the end. She was motionless, utterly exhausted by the struggle to stay alive. Her father had purchased medicine with the money he'd earned in Libya, but it was too late: Young-mi died three days later.

Next to Young-mi's empty seat sat Lee Seung-chul, another pupil I liked a lot. Seung-chul wanted to become a doctor one day and care for the children who by now were filling the streets. He was sad to have lost his classmate. Although I'd begun with a class of forty-something pupils two years earlier, fewer than twenty-five remained on my roster.

***

In May that same year, my mother came home from a trip one day and took a big apple from her bag. 'This is for *Unni*,' she told me. 'She's pregnant, she needs to eat!' *Unni*, who had just turned twenty-nine, had been working in the textile factory in Ranam for the past six years. My father had long ago given up any hope of separating her from Sang-chul. This news gave him a pretext for setting a wedding date: it would take place on 20 July 1993. In spite of everything *Unni* was thrilled and I was happy for her.

The wedding was marked by a totally unexpected presence: that of my maternal grandmother, the one who had abandoned my mother at the age of five. There she was, among the guests. It was the first time I met her. Her name was Han Sun-ja.

'How did you find her?' I whispered to Mum when no one else was looking.

'I haven't seen her since I was a child, but I tracked her down in Kimchaek with the help of some acquaintances. I decided to invite her because I wanted to show her how successful I've become without her, how proud I was of my family. Do you understand?'

'*Eomeoni* ...'

'I still resent that she abandoned me so I'm avenging myself in my own way. That's just how it is. Do you know she went and started another family and had four children after me?'

I didn't know what to say – not to my mother in that moment, nor to my grandmother the next day, when she came up to me and introduced herself. All I felt was a deep sadness, an inconsolable grief before this mother and daughter who seemed to come together and then part so haphazardly. The moment the two ageing women met each other again, both of their faces were awash with tears.

Two days later, my grandmother left: it was the first and last time we saw her.

***

All Korean mothers dream of giving their daughter a beautiful wedding. Even in the most miserable conditions they find a way to save up for this. With the money she had set aside from her business dealings, our mother actually managed to purchase a flat in the building next door to ours. This was her gift to *Unni*. According to the Confucian tradition, the bride becomes a member of the groom's family, but in this case Sang-chul's family was far too poor, so he became part of his wife's family. It wasn't exactly honourable for a man, but he had no choice.

The year 1993 was also a year of goodbyes: my sister had barely left home when it was my brother's turn to go. Jeong-ho was called up to join the army's Ninth Division. He had hoped to become a pilot in Pyongyang but he too was not spared the curse of my mother's *songbun*, and so at seventeen he found himself posted quite far from Chongjin. Separating families, sending new recruits as far from home as possible, was the State's way of eradicating family ties.

As if my brother's imminent departure hadn't created enough turmoil in our family, 1993 was also the year my mother was arrested for illegal trade. One scorchingly hot August afternoon, I was at home with her when two men came to our door. They were wearing ordinary clothing, so I didn't dream they had come to arrest someone.

'Would you please come with us to the police station?' they asked Mum. 'We have some questions we'd like to ask you.'

There were the pigs in 1978. Then the dried fish and the Chinese cigarettes … I could go on. Fifteen years of illegal business activity. There's a Korean proverb that says, 'He who has a long tail always gets caught.' My mother didn't resist and the policemen took her away. I wasn't too worried because I thought it was going to be one of those information sessions where they asked her about our uncle in the South, who was supposed to visit us. Later, when I told my father what had happened, his reaction revealed just how serious the situation was: someone in our building had denounced her for her business dealings.

We didn't know what would become of her.

On 8 August, I went to the police station to tell my mother that my brother was leaving the next day. She had terrible back pain, but in spite of that she insisted on accompanying him to the train station. She managed to negotiate a one-day release to say goodbye to her son, dried octopus having once again worked its magic. My father instructed us not to cry in front of Jeong-ho, so we all smiled widely. But our smiles only hid the unbearable pain of knowing that his military service would last ten years and most likely we wouldn't see him until he had completed it. As soon as we arrived back home, Mum was taken away by the waiting police officers, but to our great surprise they held her for only a few days. *Eomeoni* had become an expert negotiator and she made it through thanks to copious amounts of Chinese cigarettes without ever revealing a thing about her business partners. That's how she built her reputation as a trustworthy businesswoman – by never denouncing anyone.

***

On 5 February 1994, *Unni* gave birth to a baby girl and named her Soo-jung. Despite being born in difficult times, the baby received a good deal of love and attention: like an oasis in the desert, she drew everyone to her. *Unni*'s job was to find her enough to eat, my mother cleaned *Unni*'s flat, I washed the nappies and my father spent his time admiring the baby.

Soo-jung was hope, she was life.

Ever since his heart attack in 1991, *Abeoji* had lost his joie de vivre. But now, in the presence of Soo-jung, his face shone like before. I knew he had dreamed of having grandchildren, and even if he was a little disappointed not to have a grandson, he fell under his granddaughter's spell in no time. He never left her – it was as though he needed her around to maintain a zest for life.

At school I was a teacher, but with Soo-jung I got to play mummy. We even looked alike – so much so that when I took her with me on walks, people thought she was my daughter. I was so proud; I told myself that I too would someday be a mum and that my child would know her multiplication tables by the age of four – just like her mother, her uncle Jeong-ho, her aunt Myeong-sil and her cousin Soo-jung.

Spring being the season for 'excursions', I took my pupils to Onsung, at the northern tip of the Korean Peninsula, to work in the fields. It was the exact same trip I had been forced to take fifteen years earlier when I was a pupil. This part of the country, which shared a border with China and Russia, was even poorer than the area around Chongjin. I had to make the rounds of the entire village just to find enough food to feed the children dinner. Since we teachers spent our days sitting around discussing *A Century of Memories*, the biography of Kim Il-sung, we could afford to eat a bit less but our pupils were subjected to hard physical labour and needed their strength.

At around 11.30 on 8 July 1994, an unbearably hot day, my class was interrupted by the sound of a high-pitched siren. Less than five minutes later, everyone had gathered in the school's auditorium. There we found ourselves in front of the Headmaster's television set, which he had placed in the middle of the room. South Korea's President, Kim Young-sam, had just completed his official visit to the North and I wondered if the time of reunification had finally come. At high noon, the television announcer Ri Choon-hi appeared. She was dressed all in black, in a traditional *Jeogori*. Weeping, she announced,

'At 2am this morning, Dear Leader Kim Il-sung passed away.'

My legs began to tremble.

What? How is this possible? What should I do? Oh yes – cry. I have to cry. This is the only occasion when we're allowed to show our tears in public, so take advantage of it. Think of your hunger, your pain, your exhausted body, your brother whom you miss so much, think of Park Young-mi, think of Lee Seung-chul, think of all the children who have died too young. Let it go. Cry. Cry the tears to reassure yourself that we are all human. At least your tears will be sincere. You are still in touch with your emotions. Show your tears, let them think you're crying for him, for Great Leader, but weep for yourself, for your own sorrow. Everyone will see it as a sign of your exceptional loyalty to the Party.

Children and teachers, 3,000 of them, stood there, silent as a graveyard.

Suddenly, the Headmaster shook himself out of his stupor and launched into an almost mechanical frenzy of sobbing, like a robot whose 'heartbreak' button has been pressed. I started to tear up too: if I had to cry, I would cry. Soon the great hall was filled with the sound of wailing and laments and cries of 'Oh, Great Leader! Great Leader!' Some of the children had parents in prisoner camps while others had absolutely nothing to eat, yet here they were, doing their best to squeeze out some tears. It was survival instinct. The hysteria went on for an hour. When at last the Headmaster dried his eyes, he announced that classes were cancelled for the day and asked us to go express our condolences at the statue of Kim Il-sung in Pohang.

After a two-hour journey on foot, we arrived at the statue. A great crowd had already formed. Children were fainting in the heat.

For two weeks – the official period of mourning – the town more or less stopped living. There were no buses in the street, no passengers on the trains. Back in Ranam, every day at noon on the dot, *ajumma* from our flat went to pay homage to the town statue, where they observed three minutes of silence. I did the same with my students.

The funeral took place on 17 July, in Pohang. Kim Jong-Il, the fifty-two-year-old son of Kim Il-sung, became our new leader. It was the end of one reign and the beginning of another, one that would prove to be a darker form of tyranny than the one that came before.

***

Food had been in short supply even before the death of Kim Il-sung. In 1995, when I was twenty-seven, I stopped receiving a salary. I sent the few ration tickets I had to the army: it was the only means I had to help my brother.

Unni had stopped working after Soo-jung was born and she mostly took care of her daughter while serving as the *ajumma* of her building. She loved this work, but she also knew that women were no longer allowed to work in the factory once they became mothers, which is why she had taken the initiative herself. But she had trouble feeding Soo-jung and could only count on whatever her fisherman husband earned.

Most factories were shuttered due to the lack of raw materials and electricity, and my father's was no exception. At the risk of being shot for attempting to undermine Socialism, more and more people began looting factories, scavenging bits of iron, ladders, even electric cords – the copper wire inside the insulating sheath could be sold for a good price in China. Hunger drove them to make bad decisions, turning good people into criminals. They even stole the pots of kimchi that had been buried in front of the flat – until then a place we'd believed was sacred and off limits.

The water we boiled for drinking was contaminated by the waste materials from the nearby factories. The only cure for the diarrhoea caused by drinking polluted water cost 200 or 300 won on the black market – a very high price, considering a kilo of rice cost 150 won.

That 200 won was also the price of a flat, since people were forced to trade their homes for a kilo or two of rice or corn. Entire families found themselves on the street, living in unstable conditions for the rest of their days. Children as young as four and five sold biscuits in the markets, older children became wandering nomads. Some adults stole, while others died of exhaustion caused by lack of nourishment. In most cases those who fell ill never recovered – it was chaos.

***

A year later, in May 1996, my student Kwang-chul – Mrs Jang from next door's son – appeared in my office, breathless.

'*Seonsengnim*,' he said, 'Teacher, Jin and her family ...'

'I see ... Calm down, Kwang-chul. Thank you for letting me know. Go sit down now. I'll go see them after class this afternoon.'

No words were spoken. No questions asked. We all knew what was happening. Jin was Kwang-chul's best friend and he was terrified.

'*Neh*,' he answered sheepishly before returning to his seat.

Terrified, I climbed the five flights of stairs with Kwang-chul. The flat had only one bedroom, just like ours back in Ranam. Jin's family had exchanged everything they owned for rice and corn in order to stay alive. Their flat was stripped bare. They all lay on the floor, curled up next to each other. Empty bowls were scattered here and there. They looked as though they simply hadn't woken from their sleep. The building delegate told me that after wandering around for seven days without finding any food, they had let themselves die together after a final family meal: dying of hunger was certainly not an enviable way to go, but it was a way to go together.

That could be us lying there. That is not how I want Jeong-ho to find us if he comes home to visit. I don't want to die, not alone – and not as a family.

***

One day that same year, while accompanying my mother to the market in Sunam, she surprised me by handing me a rice cake she'd just bought. A rice cake in those times was unthinkable! I was just about to eat the entire thing in one bite when a little kid appeared out of nowhere, snatched it out of my hands and ran away.

A merchant who had seen the whole thing burst out laughing and said, 'See? I told you to eat privately, when no one can see. Serves you right for being careless!'

That was not the only child whom hunger had changed into a thief. The same day, on our way home, I spotted a few of my pupils hanging about, begging from stall to stall. In truth, I was surprised to see them alive – they hadn't been to class in over a year. Instead they roamed the streets in search of food. They would sneak onto trains, and as soon as the train entered a tunnel they would throw themselves on the workers' backpacks to ferret out snacks tucked in the bottom of their bags. These children were known as *Kotjebis*, 'migrating swallows'. Such birds could no longer sit in the nest waiting for mama birds to drop worms in their beaks. Instinctively, they became predators.

Standing before this crowd of children dressed in rags, I felt awkward in the well-cut blue suit my mother had brought me from China. When one of the children stuck his hand in the sewer to pick out a few grains of rice, I turned away abruptly. I couldn't bear to look at this scene any more, I was sick to the stomach with shame. Ashamed for them. Ashamed of myself. As their teacher, I had taken advantage of my influence to spread lies, telling stories to make them believe that the Kim family would protect them. I knew I was being dishonest with them. A liar, that's what I was. The sudden awareness was unbearable, but I had to accept it if I was going to live.

The next day, Seung-chul came to see me following afternoon classes:

'*Seonsengnim*, may I please be excused a little early today?'

'You know that's not possible,' I said. 'No one can miss class unless they're sick.'

I knew perfectly well why he wanted to leave early – he wanted to join the little tramps at the Sunam market. Perhaps I should have let him go, but in addition to being a liar I had become a selfish coward – I had accepted that from then on I would take care only of myself. I couldn't afford to have any more absent pupils because I would be criticised for it during our weekly meetings. I had to continue to teach in front of a ghost-class as though nothing were amiss. Above all, I had to keep my job – even without being paid.

Seung-chul never returned to my class.

My friend Hye-young was not doing well either. Her family had sold the television set and the sewing machine that her father had brought back from Russia. The few items of value that remained would carry them through winter.

Towards the middle of 1996, children began collapsing on the pavements. Resignation set in. The stench of dead bodies, people being publicly executed in the market for stealing food, soldiers who used their weapons to threaten the citizens in order to ensure their own existence – all this was now part of daily life in Ranam.

One day, while walking through the market, I spied the body of a little boy hunched against the wall. He wasn't moving. I tiptoed up to him, weaving among the passers-by who wandered aimlessly in a state of passivity. The boy's face was covered in filth, his clothing was muddy and his long hair tangled in knots. *No, not him, please, no!*

I thought. Eyes wide in despair, I covered my mouth with both hands and held my breath: it was my pupil, Lee Seung-chul. The little boy who wanted to care for the children in the street. The boy who would never become a doctor because his life had come to an end at the age of thirteen as he huddled against a wall. The little barefoot boy who still haunts me to this day.

CHAPTER TEN

Before too long, death came to call. It wasn't something that happened only to other people.

One day in August 1996, during the summer break from school, I was home alone when a colleague of *Keun Abeoji*, my father's older brother, came to visit. She worked with him on the farm at Ragwondong.

'I think your uncle is sick,' she said. 'Very sick. He hasn't come to work on the farm for two weeks.'

'Oh, no …'

'I'm very worried about him. You should go see him – now.'

No sooner had she spoken those words than she ran down the stairs, uncomfortable at being the bearer of bad news. All sorts of morbid thoughts crossed my mind as I stood in the doorway, trembling with fright. I kept checking the time, hoping my father would come home from the factory as soon as possible.

'Father, someone's been to visit me. *Keun Abeoji* isn't well,' I said the moment he walked in.

Abeoji paused on the threshold and sighed deeply. Then, looking stern but composed, he asked me to make some soup: 'a light broth,' he specified, 'something easy to digest'. Then he disappeared. The sound of his footsteps as he ran down the stairs spoke volumes about his frantic state. The farm was an hour's walk away, there wasn't a moment to lose.

Four hours passed before I heard his steps again. It was 10pm; he had carried *Keun Abeoji* the entire way home on his back. He was utterly exhausted. Too tired to speak, he indicated the bedroom with his chin. I scurried ahead to spread a blanket on the floor so he could place *Keun Abeoji* on it. This was our father's older brother, our 'big' uncle, yet he had never seemed so small. Gone were the muscular shoulders and arms he'd once been so proud of, now he was nothing more than skin and bones. Unrecognisable.

Keun Abeoji, how can this be?

'I'm hungry ...' he moaned, staring into space. 'So hungry ...'

I didn't understand how someone who worked on a farm could have found himself with nothing to eat. It made no sense. Didn't he grow corn?

In the hot, humid night air, his clothing clung to his skin, revealing how emaciated he was.

'Why didn't you come to us sooner?' asked my father, irritated. 'Why didn't you ask for help? Why?'

'I'm so hungry...'

Abeoji took the bowl I had prepared and placed a spoonful of broth in his brother's mouth. Then another, and another. In less than five minutes, there was nothing left.

'More ...' *Keun Abeoji* murmured, staring at the empty bowl.

To hear my uncle plead like that broke my heart. I was on my way back to the kitchen to get more soup when my father blocked my path.

'Absolutely not! It's dangerous to give him too much food all at once. We have to wait, we have to let him sleep now. Tomorrow morning, we'll give him a little more. You should go to sleep, too – you must be tired.'

It was a night of anguish. I rose the next morning with a heavy heart. It was 5.30am. *Abeoji* was already at his brother's bedside, his brow furrowed, a look of remorse and guilt in his eyes. Then, composing himself, he told his brother:

'Rest now. I have to go to the factory but Jihyun will take care of you. See you this evening.'

All day I tended to *Keun Abeoji*. I wiped his body with a moistened cloth to cool his rough skin that was covered with blisters; I crushed the lice hidden in his clothing. I gave him a bowl of broth at midday and another at the end of the day. That evening, he fell asleep before my father returned.

The next morning, while preparing to make breakfast for *Abeoji*, I noticed that the bowl of soup I'd left in the kitchen was empty. I rushed into the room to find *Keun Abeoji* groaning on the floor, then I ran to tell my father.

'*Abeoji, Abeoji*, come quickly,' I said, throwing open the door to his room. '*Keun Abeoji* has drunk the bowl of broth that was in the kitchen!'

My father was awake and sitting up on his mat. Knowing that this could mean death, he pursed his lips and shook his head. Suddenly he jumped up, threw on the trousers that were now too big for him and ran into the room where his brother lay. Sitting on the floor next to him, he took *Keun Abeoji*'s head in his hands. Tears fell on my uncle's sunken cheeks.

'*Hyungnim*,' he said, his voice tender, wistful and kind. He loved and respected his brother. This was the handicapped brother their dying mother had entrusted him with.

Over the next few days, *Abeoji* spoke to his brother this way every morning before leaving for the factory, telling him how badly he had failed in his duties despite the promises he had made to their mother.

Day after day, we remained powerless to ease my uncle's suffering. On the sixth day, he became calm but refused to eat. I understood that he no longer wanted to try – he was too tired, his stomach rejected all food. His throat closed, allowing nothing to get through. He sought our eyes, looking from me to my father and back again. He shed one tear and then took his final breath in the arms of my father. After that, utter silence.

There was no wooden coffin, so my uncle's body was wrapped in straw, placed in an ox-drawn cart and taken to Mount Nongpo. That was where we had buried my grandmother, *Halmeoni*. If anyone asked, we told them my uncle died of measles, that he had caught the childhood disease late in life: one does not die of hunger in a socialist country.

CHAPTER TEN

After my uncle's death, something in my family changed forever. My father began to openly insult the Party, saying, 'Those rats are lying to us about the state our country is in!'

My sister *Unni* did the same – she spent every week working alongside the *ajummas* from our block of flats without ever having the right to complain about how hard it was to feed her little girl, Soo-jung, who was now four years old.

A few weeks later, it was our old neighbour Mrs Jang's turn to depart. That kind woman who used to come and help my mother cook when we had family get-togethers had sold everything she owned and now lived in a flat that contained only a television set in the middle of the bedroom. There was no electricity so the telly served no purpose, but it had been a gift of the government, so it couldn't be sold. It was on that television that we had watched propaganda movies as kids! Those were the days …

In the autumn of 1996, both Mrs Jang and her 23-year-old daughter died of the 'disease'.

***

Competition was growing stiffer in the dried-fish business and it was difficult to come out on top. My mother had to give up her own business and try another sector. This time she would leverage luxury items – antique vases, silk screens, leather goods, things that would appeal to rich people. There were lots of rich people in China.

Thanks to her reputation as a solid businesswoman, Mum was able to obtain a loan of 3,000 won to get her business off the ground. The money came from 'Koreans from Japan', whom we called *Jae-il Kyopo*. These were Koreans who had left home and gone to Japan between 1910 and 1945, during the Japanese occupation, in the hope of a better life. In the 1960s, Japan encouraged them to try their chances in North Korea, which they depicted as a sort of El Dorado. Those who went did in fact live a rather good life. You could identify them right away by their handsome clothes and accent. They were moneylenders who made it rich on the backs of the poor by charging exorbitant interest rates. My mother thought that her partners from the fish business would buy her luxury goods, but that was not to be: she lost all the money she had borrowed and soon went into debt.

For a whole month the creditors came to our home twice a day. My mother went underground. She would leave the flat very early in the morning and not return until late in the evening to avoid running into them. They could be heard cursing her in the hallways, putting the whole building on high alert. My father, completely depressed, never left the flat any more. The creditors began to take away our furniture and kitchen equipment. Our flat was being emptied out and so was my heart.

On 18 April 1997, my mother left for Onsung, a city on the eastern point of the peninsula, near China and Russia – she couldn't keep living underground. She starting talking about a distant cousin of hers who lived in China:

'Onsung is the only place where I can try phoning her,' she told us before she left. 'I'm sure she can help me get my business up and running again.'

'But who exactly is this cousin?' I asked.

'A distant family member I got in touch with in the eighties. I don't know where exactly she is in China, I'll have to look for her. You take care of your father. I'll be back in a few days, once I've found her.'

She asked me several times to take good care of *Abeoji*.

Was she going to come back?

***

'Where is your mother? Where is she ...?'

Abeoji had just had his second heart attack. He no longer got out of bed. In his delirium, he called out for his wife all day long.

'Don't worry, she'll be back in a few weeks,' I told him.

CHAPTER TEN

I was furious. I'd been given responsibility for my father without having been asked. We had neither money nor ration tickets, and every day I had to figure out a way to put a bowl of rice on the table for him. On 30 April 1997, I handed in my official resignation at school in order to care for him full-time. It was a heart-wrenching decision, because even without having been paid for the past three years I still loved my job. The idea of abandoning the children broke my heart, but the idea of having to beg for food was even worse.

I searched for food on Mount Nongpo. Roots, plants, mushrooms, bark ... I gathered anything that could be ground up to serve as a base for broth. Maranta root, for example. It was rare, but its nutritional value was greater than that of any other root, which made it highly desirable. I just had to remember to soak the roots in water before cooking them to rid them of their poison. We also ate the inside of pine bark, which I boiled and cut into pieces before serving. I was used to working the earth – Mrs Jang had taught me to distinguish between plants and weeds – so somehow I got by. However, I couldn't get rid of the feeling of humiliation that had seeped into me since I had shifted into survival mode. I walked along the railway tracks looking for grasses and I dug in the rice fields looking for shoots. I had been a teacher. My father had worked in a factory his whole life. We had been one of the few families who could afford to eat white rice every day. Living on grasses and roots was hard to swallow.

My uncle had died of hunger, my father was near death himself, and I was living like a rat, scrounging in the dirt for something to eat.

Like a machine that's been programmed at the factory and won't stop, I heard myself say, *This is the West's fault! They are the ones who imposed sanctions on us! We live in a socialist country, where no one should die of hunger!* But necessity makes us do strange things: no matter how hard I tried to resist it, I'd been brainwashed. What a powerful weapon for a people who, to ensure its very existence, would cling to anything to justify their fate to themselves.

By June 1997, even the hills had nothing left to offer: the villagers had stripped them bare. What were we to do now? There was only one thing left, and that was to sell what was in the wooden chest in the bedroom: school diplomas that my father had carefully saved, the maths book that *Unni* had copied by hand, *Abeoji's* black Party uniform, my dark-blue wool teacher's suit.

'*Abeoji*, I'm sorry to cause you this pain, but I must sell your uniform,' I said. 'I know what it means to you. I'm so sorry, I have no choice.'

My father watched me, his face drawn.

'No need to answer. I can see you understand,' I told him as I gathered the items.

I sold the uniform and my suit to the first comer for 220 won: the price of three eggs and a kilogram of cornmeal, enough to feed my father and me for a month. Though pleased and proud of my achievement, I was also saddened as I thought about how my mother had suffered her entire life just to put a bowl of rice on the table for her family.

On 27 July 1997, we were told at a teachers' meeting that the sanctions imposed by the West were directly responsible for the famine and that our country had been invaded by spies who were manipulating the economy. According to the delegate of our block of flats, hundreds of executions had taken place by the Suseong River. Seo Gwan-hee, the minister of agriculture at the time, had been accused of spying for the Americans and was one of the first victims of the 'spy hunt'. He was stoned to death in public. The incident was so significant it was dubbed 'the massacre of *Simhwajo*'.

That same year, my father had his third heart attack. He had a hard time recovering because the food I managed to find was not enough to restore his strength. Pale, he began to complain of stomach pain.

Oh, no, not that! Hang in there, Abeoji. I'm here for you. Hang in there.

In my mind I replayed the scene of our uncle languishing before our eyes. I remembered every detail with precision. Stomach pain was a bad sign. I began to despair. And still my mother did not come home.

***

Abeoji's condition didn't improve. By October, when my brother Jeong-ho came home to visit, he was too weak even to go to the toilet. I had to leave a metal bucket next to him.

We hadn't seen Jeong-ho for three years. Now twenty-one, he was tall and slender, and looked exactly like our father when he was young. He forced himself to hide his shock when he saw the state our father was in.

He listened to me.

He measured his words.

He kept his emotions in check.

Then he thanked me for everything I was doing for *Abeoji* and without delay prepared to leave.

'I'm going to sleep at my friend Sung-jin's place.'

'All right. Will we see you tomorrow?'

'Of course you will. I'll be back in the morning.'

Sung-jin lived in a flat about a ten-minute walk from ours. I understood that my brother wanted to go see his childhood friend, but I was a little hurt that he seemed to prefer Sung-jin's company to ours. On the other hand, I told myself that he was right: who would want to stay in this squalid place, this hovel that had been stripped bare?

So my brother spent his nights at Sung-jin's but came home every day to keep our father company. He gently massaged his arms and legs and tenderly held his hand. *Abeoji* couldn't bear for his son to look at him, he was too ashamed.

One afternoon, barely three days after his arrival, two soliders, both in their thirties, came to our door.

'We are looking for Park Jeong-ho,' they said in a Pyong-yang accent.

Soldiers often went on leave as a group, and I thought to myself that they must be in my brother's battalion.

'He's not here,' I said. 'He told me he was spending the day at his friend Sung-jin's place.'

As I closed the door, I felt the weight of someone's gaze on me: it was *Abeoji*, his eyes filled with terror. The next instant, stomach cramps racked my body. Shuddering violently, I suddenly understood that Jeong-ho had deserted the army and I had revealed his hiding place.

We were awakened at one in the morning by knocking. That night, my sister and her daughter, Soo-jung, were with us. They'd got into the habit of sleeping over when Sang-chul went fishing at night. At the door was Jeong-ho, his face bloodied, held up by the same two soldiers who had come by that afternoon. This time they each held a stick – a metre-long piece of wood you'd use to frame a door or a window. Clearly, Jeong-ho had already been beaten: he could barely stand up.

I held the door open with one hand and cried, '*Unni*, come quickly!'

'Jihyun, what's happening?' It was my father, his voice surprisingly strong, who answered instead of my sister.

Unni came to the door and, trying to sound calm, asked,

'Why have you done this to our brother?'

The soldiers didn't bother to answer. Pushing past us, they dragged Jeong-ho into the main room. They told us not to follow them. An irrepressible wave of repulsion went through me, a great shudder shook my entire body. Out of the corner of my eyes, I could see *Abeoji's* livid face. We were filled with terror.

Hearing Jeong-ho's muffled cries, I suspected that he was trying to scream in silence so as not to frighten *Abeoji* and Soo-jung, but he couldn't mask the sound of the sticks beating his body.

'Who do you think you are, eh?' shouted one of the soldiers. 'Where did you think you were going? Son-of-a-bitch!'

The row lasted for hours. From time to time I could hear a weak 'I don't know'. Soo-jung woke up and started to cry. *Unni* stayed calm and managed to rock her back to sleep in her arms. I left them in the corridor and took refuge in the kitchen, where I paced endlessly.

They're going to kill him, I thought.

At 5am, one of the soldiers came out of the room and signalled for me to clean it. I expected to find a dead body, but in spite of the pool of blood spreading across the floor I was relieved to see Jeong-ho was still alive.

Immediately after that, my brother was sent back to Pyong-yang and condemned to death. His crime: desertion.

***

'Jeong-ho has escaped again.'

'Oh my God! Tell me everything, please tell me.'

My brother's friend Sung-jin couldn't speak freely then because there were spies throughout our block of flats, but three days later he talked to me at the market in Ranam.

Travelling back to Pyong-yang by train, my brother had managed to jump from the carriage during a power cut. He was back in Ranam and staying this time with Sung-jin's grandmother.

***

My mother was being hunted down by creditors, my brother by the State. As for the rest of us in Ranam, we felt less and less safe. One day my brother-in-law, Sang-chul, his face expressionless, calmly said,

'We have to leave this country.'

In an attempt to lessen my shock, *Unni*, one of the few people in the world I trusted, took me aside and explained that we couldn't go on living like this.

'It's the only way to save Jeong-ho,' she explained. 'And if Jeong-ho gets arrested, we all get arrested. You know how it goes.'

'Where would we go?'

'China.'

'But where in China?'

'For the time being, we'll go to Onsung, near the border, and wait for our chance to cross into China. Your brother-in-law has been preparing this trip for months. He's already crossed from Onsung into China several times, just to get the lay of the land. He's even been in contact with Mother. She's waiting for us. We're going to say that you're going to marry someone from there. Sung-jin will tell Jeong-ho where we are and he'll come and join us.'

'And we'll do this with what money?'

'We'll sell the silk throws that Mum gave us for our wedding.'

'What about *Abeoji*?'

There was silence. An unbearable silence that no one dared to break for a long time.

On 18 February 1997, Sang-chul, Soo-jung and I left Ranam.

CHAPTER ELEVEN

'*Abeoji* …'

I place a bowl of rice beside you, along with a clean pair of pyjamas.

'Don't worry, our uncle *Jageun Abeoji* is coming to take care of you. I'll lock the door behind me and put the key in the kimchi pot in front of the flat.

'*Unni*, Soo-jung and I are leaving.'

I know you caught the conversation when *Unni* and Sang-chul told me we were leaving. You pretended not to be listening, but I know you heard. Just as I heard the few words you were able to murmur in your delirium. You can be sure I will find Jeong-ho, just as you asked me to do, and I will take care of him for the rest of my life. That's a promise.

Your body is hovering between life and death. You want to break free and escape this nightmare, but if you die before we go your death will weigh on our conscience, so you choose to stay alive. It's an act that speaks volumes about you, *Abeoji*. I don't know anyone in the world who is so strong, capable of such sacrifice.

This evening, everything feels peaceful. The famine seems a distant thing, as though there aren't really people in the street dying of hunger in immutable silence. In our house, all that remains are the portraits of Kim Il-sung and Kim Jong-Il hanging side by side, their biographies sitting on the bare shelves, and you, lying on your mat on the floor.

Alone. I am all alone beside you. I look at you and beg your forgiveness. I don't know if you hear me, I don't know if you see me.

Despite your dull skin and drawn features, your face is handsome. It shimmers in the darkness. *Abeoji*, I'm weeping.

Whether at home or at school, I've always managed to put on a brave face, to be a fighter. But tonight, for the first time in thirty years, I let my tears flow. They are tears of despair. Dearest Father, whom I have loved more than anything in this world, I have to leave you.

I place my hand in your stiff, cold palm. Your skin awakens slightly under my touch but I sense your distress, a boundless, inexpressible abandonment. Your half-open mouth refuses to close, your empty gaze betrays great fear. Every breath you draw is followed by a ragged exhalation.

Seeing you like this scares me, my inability to help you tears me apart. I haven't had time yet to become afraid, but my heart is seized with misery and dread. I fear these words that burn my eyes are turning into a farewell letter …

> I don't know when I stopped looking at the sky. The last time I did, I must have been eight years old. You were telling us the tale of *Haenim and Dalnim*. It's the story of how the sun and moon came into being long, long ago, even before there were stars. In that enchanted atmosphere, you and I played draughts while *Unni* and Jeong-ho played hide-and-seek. In that moment, it was as though we forgot we were hungry …
>
> Do you remember the blackouts? We would all gather by candlelight in the same room. We didn't talk, but we were together, and the darkness didn't scare us. We would go to bed early so as not to use up the candle. But when we didn't have homework, we would huddle together and light our lamp, which consisted of a tin can containing some oil and a wick. The next morning, everyone's upper lip would be smudged with soot and we'd point at each other and roar with laughter. Those light-hearted

moments, that knowing laughter – just the memory of it helps me get up in the morning, day after day.

I'm not afraid of death, no. But my childhood? I miss it. I miss *you*.

Why is it that life's sweet moments fade so easily, crushed under the weight of painful, lasting memories forever entombed in our broken hearts?

For almost eight years, time has sat heavily on your frail shoulders. For almost eight years, despite coming home from work exhausted, you've refused to eat your rice, claiming not to be hungry, nudging your bowl discreetly towards us.

Even those rolls that the restaurant *Galmaegi* in Chongjin gave you in exchange for your labour – you didn't eat those, either. You kept them carefully wrapped in your handkerchief so you could give them to us once you got home.

Last year, winter was more bitterly cold than any I'd ever known. One day it was minus 28, and I had to cover my head with a heavy cloth to protect myself from the wind. When I came home from the markets, I found your bowl of corn once again untouched. You said, 'How can I eat, knowing that you are out there freezing in the cold?'

I know it isn't hunger that has caused your decline. I saw tears of sorrow in your eyes when our mother left, tears of distress when Jeong-ho returned home covered in blood. It's this anguish that's killing you. You used to stroke my hair and tell me I was as strong and brave as any man and that you were proud of me. All my life I have sensed the tenderness you feel for me. And all my life, that is what enabled me to hang on.

When I got my teaching job, you wanted to have a drink in my honour. A bottle of rice wine cost as much as food for three meals, but I bought you one anyway, along with a bit of tofu. You took one swallow, then another, then another – slowly, as though your throat suffered with every drop of alcohol that entered your body. Your tears drowned in your glass that evening, but at 6am the next morning you were already in the kitchen, the window panes covered in steam: 'There's not enough food for me to make you a lunch to take with you, but I made you some broth. And take this …' you said, handing me a bowl. Then you gave me wrinkled bit of paper, a ration ticket. 'Take care of yourself and never, ever skip a meal. This should be enough for lunch today.'

I knew perfectly well it was a ticket you'd been holding on to in case you ran out of food someday. But I couldn't refuse it. The joy of receiving gifts from one's parents … it's a pure, undying joy that only children lucky enough to have kind and noble parents can know. I'm blessed to be among those children. I had promised myself I would take care of you forever, and yet, as you know, children are never as good as their parents. How many nights did you forgo your own sleep as you pressed cold compresses to our fevered foreheads? How many times did you feed us spoonfuls of rice even as your own stomach cried out for food? And then one day your brother died in your arms. A few weeks later, you were no longer getting out of bed. You started to dread the mornings, preferring to spend the day lying down, alone in the silence enclosed by the four walls of your room.

I tried everything to keep us alive – dried tree bark, the roots of dead plants, dust-coloured insects and frozen potatoes.

But today, I have reached my limit.

I spend every waking moment wondering how I'm going to survive, how I'm going to feed you. I can't bring myself to tell *Unni* that I have to beg for food in the street.

I daren't ask her for even a few noodles, I'm too ashamed. You wondered why your brother *Keun Abeoji* allowed himself to die in secret instead of asking you for help. Honestly, I believe I would have done the same thing.

Day is breaking.

'*Save Jeong-ho, save Jeong-ho.*'

These words are with me always.

I know that you are fighting death with every breath you take. It's a miracle that you are keeping yourself alive, I see that. I beg of you, even after you hear the door close behind us, keep going. Don't close your eyes for too long. Fight off the sleep of death, resist the heavy sadness pressing on your eyelids until we come back.

In exchange for my promise to you, I would like you to promise me something: take care of yourself. If I never see you again, you know that I will never forgive myself.

Lovingly,
Your daughter Jihyun

CHAPTER TWELVE

I knew nothing about the Chinese apart from what I had read in the history books at school. Many of them had fled to North Korea during the sixties and they had shown us their gratitude ever since. I wasn't afraid of China, especially since people there ate meat and eggs every day, according to my brother-in-law, Sang-chul. On the other hand, I *was* afraid of being caught crossing the border. I comforted myself by remembering that Sang-chul had had a lot of experience, having done it many times: he was a veteran, and I could trust him.

On 28 February 1998, after paying the driver two packs of cigarettes and 200 won, *Unni*, Sang-chul, Soo-jung and I climbed into the back of an open truck. There must have been thirty or forty of us crammed in back there.

My niece, Soo-jung, sat motionless. Her face ashen, she clutched her mother's hands. Her child's intuition told her not to move. After a long silence, the truck suddenly roared to life. Jostling all of us on board, it turned onto a bumpy mountain road. The wind whipped our bare cheeks. *Unni's* face was blue from fear and cold.

At eleven in the morning that same day, we arrived in Komusan, a town located high in the mountains north of Chongjin. We climbed out of the truck to have our papers inspected at a checkpoint.

'Where are you going?' one of the secret police officers asked *Unni*.

'My sister's going to marry a man in Onsung,' she replied calmly, showing the man the embroidered blankets she had brought along as a dowry for the fake marriage my family had concocted.

I was impressed by how inventive they were.

To our immense relief, the policemen believed her right away and let us pass. The journey, which was turning out to be long and arduous, included a stop in Hoeryong and from there a train ride to Onsung. The road was winding and seemed to go on forever. The trip took eight hours. Eight hours to get to Hoeryong, where we arrived exhausted and starving.

The dead of winter, it had snowed that evening. We could feel the snow under our feet as we made our way to that night's lodging. On every street corner I saw children dressed in rags, their faces gaunt, skin rough and their hair coated in a thick layer of grey dust. They were begging despite the bitter cold. Nothing – not even the darkness – could tear my eyes from this scene.

We spent the night in a room Sang-chul had rented for 100 won.

'I hope that *Jaguen Abeoji* will take care of Father,' I whispered to *Unni* as soon as we came in out of the cold.

As Soo-jung looked at us, trying to understand, *Unni* answered me with a silence that said it all. It was one of those moments where she didn't need to say anything, her tears of exhaustion spoke for her.

***

The next day, we caught the train to Onsung. It was supposed to pull in at 3pm, but it didn't arrive until five. Because of that, passengers who had tickets on two different trains would have to pile into one. There were neither enough seats nor tickets to buy. Nevertheless, as soon as they heard the train whistle, the crowd of people rushed towards the quay – and so did we. The carriage was full and we were bracing ourselves to spend the train ride standing up when, miracle of miracles, we found a few spots on a wooden bench on which we huddled together, overtaken by sleepiness and fatigue. The windows on the train were broken, and the icy wind that blew in froze our noses and ears, but the fear of being caught travelling without a ticket – the punishment for which was two or three days of prison camp – kept us awake and took our minds off the cold.

Finally, three hours later, at 8pm, we arrived safe and sound at our destination, Onsung – the first part of our journey that had lasted forty-eight hours. Beyond the snowy plains that ran alongside the frozen Tumen River rose a range of white-capped mountains.

We spent two days in the flat of the smuggler that my brother-in-law had found for us, waiting for the right moment to cross the border. I didn't know how Sang-chul had managed to arrange all this, but I felt very grateful to him.

A bridge built under the Japanese occupation connected Onsung to China. It was narrow and about 30 metres long. Korean soldiers guarded one side of the border, Chinese guards policed the other. There was only one way to get to China: by swimming across the river. Or rather, by walking across it, because it was frozen. The Yalu River, which runs along the rest of North Korea's border with China, runs deep with a swift current. Luckily, this particular stretch of the Tumen was shallow and narrow. We prayed that on the day of our crossing the ice would not give in under our feet.

At the end of those two days, on 21 February 1998, the time to act finally came. It was just after midnight, and the banks of the river were engulfed in utter darkness.

'Follow me,' said Sang-chul in a calm, measured voice. 'Whatever you do, don't let me out of your sight.'

My sister and niece were mute with fear; they hadn't spoken a word all day. Holding our breath, we followed the smuggler, a tall young man in his twenties. We slipped through the cornfields towards the river. Using a stick, the smuggler cleared a path in the snow. He was exceedingly cautious, careful not to break the tomb-like silence that reigned over the fields. After fifteen minutes of walking in darkness we arrived at the border, but instead of the barbed wire and guards I had been expecting I found myself before a flat sandbank encased in ice: the Tumen River, frozen. We would have to cross it on foot to reach the promised land.

CHAPTER TWELVE

We knew that soldiers were on duty at all hours, so we had to move quickly. The smuggler took the lead, followed by Sang-chul, carrying his daughter on his shoulders, then *Unni*. I brought up the rear. My face pale under the black sky, I moved unsteadily, like a baby who is just learning to walk, taking one step at a time, wishing I could make the night last longer. Hardly daring to breathe, I didn't look back. The icy air had turned my clothes into sheets of snow that clung to my skin. I was frozen right down to my bones, but we had to reach the hill on the other side before daybreak.

As I walked, I focused on each step so as not to slip. This also helped me forget my fear. But I couldn't help wondering how many innocent souls had been swallowed up by this river; how many had managed to cross the twenty-some metres of frozen water and reach China; how many had abandoned their father on his deathbed, a bowl of cold rice beside him?

***

Fifteen minutes. It took us fifteen minutes to cross from one world into another. We had just set foot on Chinese soil when we heard the Korean guards behind us shouting, 'Fugitives!' We also heard gunshots, but it was too late: we were out of range. We weren't very far from the river, but we had arrived on the Chinese side. We didn't pause to catch our breath or rejoice at having made it across; Sang-chul had paid off the smuggler and we were henceforth on our own. We ran towards the first house we saw. Sang-chul knocked on the door and a Chinese woman opened it. Despite our muddy rags, our skin and hair stiff with cold and our wan faces, she invited us in.

She served us soup and eggs with white rice on the side. It was the first egg I had eaten since selling my suit at the market. I thought of my father. In Korea, we had lived with death for years, yet just across the border another world existed. A world barely 100 metres away, where you could bask in abundance.

A middleman whom Sang-chul had contacted came the next morning at 8am. It was the same man, he said, who had received my mother a few months earlier when she had arrived in China alone. Sang-chul trusted him. He was fleshy and wore a leather jacket. We all got in his car and he brought us to Tumen, a small city in Jilin Province.

'Welcome to China!' he shouted, turning back to face us. 'You've freed yourselves from the grip of that bastard, Kim Jong-Il!'

Unni and I looked at each other, terrified – we didn't dare move a muscle the entire trip.

Openly speaking out against Kim Jong-Il? Incredible! China really is another world ...

The middleman brought us to Tumen, where his wife invited us into their flat. Ever since crossing the border, we had received a warm reception by the Chinese who took us in. It was not until this woman told us we were never to leave the flat that our faith was shaken. If we aroused the neighbours' suspicion and they denounced us, we'd be sent back to North Korea for sure. That was when I had a feeling that things in China weren't going to go as planned.

The reality was that the Chinese did not offer me their friendship, nor they did not grant me refugee status. What I had taken for gestures of generosity had been nothing more than acts of self-interest in the form of financial transactions. In the end, we were merely illegal immigrants to them. Was this really an improvement over what we'd left behind? I wasn't so sure.

Jeong-ho joined us at last two weeks later, having made the same journey to Tumen that we had. He asked us for news of *Abeoji*. When my brother saw that *Unni* and I could not bring ourselves to answer him, he understood. His face froze. He couldn't hide his expression, a mixture of contempt and anguish. To this very day, my blood freezes in my veins when I picture that scene: silence is sometimes crueller than the harshest words.

After leaving Tumen, we spent three weeks in Hunchun, where we stayed with a journalist friend of Sang-chul's, before moving on to Milgang, where my mother had been living for the past few months. It was mid-March and spring was in the air in Heilongjiang Province but my reunion with *Eomeoni* was not exactly what I had prepared myself for.

She was living in a small house in the country with, to my great surprise, a Chinese man named Mr Han. He barely greeted us. My mother flashed us a smile as she rushed towards Soo-jung and took her in her arms. *Eomeoni* had gained weight. While *Abeoji* had lain in bed dying of hunger, she had been living comfortably with this man for almost a year. I felt anger rise in me. Trembling, barely able to breathe, I said:

'*Eomeoni*, why? Why haven't you asked us about Father? Do you … do you at least have some idea of what condition he's in? Do you have any idea? Any idea at all?'

Surprised by my outburst, she didn't answer me. Instead she kept her attention focused on Soo-jung.

'*Eomeoni!* I'm talking to you!' I persisted. '*Abeoji* asked about you night and day for twelve months! *Twelve months!* And just look at the life you've been leading!'

Jeong-ho was just as furious as I was, but rather than lose his temper he took me aside and in a low voice said, '*Noona*, let it go! Something's not right. Let's drop it for now, we'll try to find out more in the morning.'

His words calmed me. I felt a little reassured.

'Come to the table, children,' said *Eomeoni*, ushering us into the main room of the house. 'I've made you pork, fish, eggs and potatoes. I hope you like it. As for your father, I know he's sick, and I know it hasn't been easy for you all. I'm sorry.'

She actually remarried, started a new life while we were at death's door every single day, and now she says she's sorry? Who's she kidding?

I was beside myself. My eyes were shooting daggers. It was then that I noticed her forced smile and the uneasiness that she was having a great deal of trouble hiding. Maybe Jeong-ho was right;

maybe there was more to the situation. Maybe there was something she couldn't reveal in front of Mr Han.

At that late hour, the sight of food had transformed us into wild animals and under *Eomeoni's* benevolent gaze we ate in complete silence except for the *tink* of chopsticks and spoons against the bowls. For a few seconds, even her fake smile seemed to fade away.

The meal lasted half an hour. No sooner had we finished eating than my mother turned to me and said, 'Jiyhun, I have something to tell you. Tomorrow, you must leave.'

'What do you mean, leave tomorrow? To go where?'

'There are far more of us than this little house can hold. The neighbours will suspect something. And you know that if they denounce us we'll all be sent back to North Korea immediately.'

Then, looking me straight in the eyes, she said firmly, 'You must leave in order to save your brother and sister.'

'But why me?' I said. 'And where would I go? This is crazy!'

'We need money,' she told me, her voice hoarse and trembling. 'Here in China, young Korean women are in demand. Single Chinese men outnumber the women.'

Desperately, I looked around the room, hoping to find a reassuring look, but all I saw were downcast eyes.

Everything was starting to become clear – *Unni's* gentle words as she told me we were leaving for China, the subtle looks she'd exchanged with her husband. This had been the plan since the beginning, and my mother had been in the know. My sister hadn't lied to the police officers in Komusan: the marriage was not fake, I had been tricked.

I had a sudden urge to vomit. I began to hiccup and sob at the same time. Fortunately, Jeong-ho broke the silence: 'She is *not* going to marry a Chinese man! She's Korean!' he shouted, horrified. 'She'll work in the fields with us, like everyone else. You can't seriously mean you're selling her to a Chinese man!'

But *Eomeoni* and Sang-chul were unmoved by Jeong-ho's protests and they began to argue bitterly.

If only I had known, if only I had known … I never would have left Korea, I would not have abandoned Abeoji. *He at least would have protected me. He would never have permitted such a scheme.*

Suddenly Jeong-ho stood up and punched Sang-chul in the stomach. Then he grabbed a knife and began to threaten him. Summoning all the strength of her fifty-three years, my mother managed to separate them. All the while, Mr Han looked on indifferently as Soo-jung cried by herself in a corner. *Unni*'s face showed neither anger nor indignation. She had been in on it, there was no reason for her to be shocked. Her eyes brimming with tears, she seized Soo-jung's hand and dragged her into the next room.

I had never before hated someone so intensely. All my life I had trusted my sister – how was this possible?

My mother took me aside and said, 'The money this marriage will bring in will save our family. We will be grateful to you to the end of our days. You'll see, you're not the only North Korean woman to marry a Chinese man. Some of them are happily married. Don't worry too much …'

My brother interrupted her, 'Little *Noona*, don't listen to her. You mustn't leave us!'

But I had no words: I was split between growing hatred for my sister and overwhelming love for my brother. And as I always did in moments of great distress, I thought of my father: '*Save Jeong-ho. Save Jeong-ho.*' *It's my mission*, I thought to myself. *I will never forget my mission. Don't worry,* Abeoji. *Of course I'll take care of my brother.*

Sometimes the smallest thing can tip you over to one side or the other. Sometimes it's just two little words: '*Save Jeong-ho.*'

I had to save my brother, and for that I had to bring in a lot of money.

The next morning, while I was expecting my mother to take me to meet my future Chinese husband, Mr Han's cousin came to get me. Everything happened so smoothly, it made me think Mr Han had been an accomplice as well. His cousin was a rather short woman. She didn't tell me her name but she acted friendly towards me. She offered to come with me to downtown Mudanjiang to begin the marriage 'procedure'. I left Mr Han's house without saying goodbye to anyone.

***

In the car that was taking me to Mudanjiang, a city in the southeastern part of Heilongjiang Province, I thought to myself that if my mother had not taken up with Mr Han – and I didn't know the terms of their 'cohabitation' – we probably wouldn't have had a place to house Jeong-ho and *Unni's* family. Having failed to get a new business off the ground as she had promised to do when she left Korea a year earlier, at least Mum had managed to figure out a way to house her family and a new way to make money … at my expense. Her reasoning was logical: having one less mouth to feed would be helpful at that time. On the other hand, she doubtless had no idea how everything would eventually turn out, and one thing seemed clear to me: she had made a grave mistake.

An unforgivable one.

In Mudanjiang, a short bald man in his forties invited us into his two-room flat. Chinese of North Korean descent, his name was Sung-jin Hwang, but he went by the name of Jogyo. He spoke Korean with a strong Onsung accent. His wife, also North Korean, was young and very beautiful. There were two little boys playing in one room and three young women in the other.

The women were North Korean. Their high cheekbones gave them away. What were they doing there? What were they waiting for? Huddled together in a corner of the room, they avoided my eyes. I didn't say a word to them either – I was well aware that anonymity was important in this type of situation.

Isolated in that sordid flat, I lived through three days of anguish in the company of my compatriots with no idea what I was doing there until the day Jogyo called me into his bedroom. It was the first time I was alone with him. When he locked the door behind me, suddenly I understood.

I understood the distress and hopelessness I'd seen on the faces of those three women in the next room the day I had arrived. I had mistaken their expression for one of indifference and distrust. In fact, they had already suffered the indignity that I was about to endure: they were desperate.

I knew that something terrible was about to happen to me and that no one was coming to save me.

'If you put up a fight, I'll denounce you,' I was told.

Rage – deep, cold, white – consumed me. Squeezing my hands into fists, I told myself I would face every obstacle and every torment, that I was afraid of nothing, and that I would protect my brother at any price.

***

When your body is no longer yours, it's your soul that guides you. My soul remained true, truer than ever. It suffered no damage but remained pure, intact; it had been soiled by a betrayal, that of my mother and sister. Traumatic as it was, what Jogyo inflicted on me was nothing compared to the magnitude of the pain that betrayal caused me: it is a wound that neither reason nor time has healed.

***

The next day, Jogyo's wife took me to the public baths in town. While I washed myself, she looked me up and down as though she were evaluating a piece of merchandise before setting it out on a shelf to sell. She told me she had undergone the same fate a few years back and that by luck – bad luck, perhaps – Jogyo had decided to keep her on as his wife and given her two children. I didn't envy her despite what seemed like her 'established' position – I told myself I would know a better fate.

The following day, Jogyo took me to a sort of exhibition hall where an auction was taking place. There were all types of merchandise: old women, ugly women, handicapped women, young girls. It was not simply a market where men came to buy women. Entire families came to purchase workers – slaves to plough their fields instead of oxen. The young twenty-somethings sold for 10,000 yuan. Those between thirty and forty were worth 5-8,000, and the skinny ones less than five.

The whole time that I was held in Jogyo's house, I travelled to and from this market whenever there were potential clients. It wasn't until two months later that one of the organisers contacted Jogyo to tell him he had a buyer.

'Park Jihyun!'

'4,000 yuan!' cried an old man standing among the buyers.

'5,000, but that's it!' shouted an olive-skinned man in a blue jacket and black trousers. 'She doesn't look too sturdy. Look at her ankles, they're too slender to work in the fields. She's not worth 1 yuan over 5,000!'

'If you don't think she's worth more than that, why don't you go buy someone else?' Jogyo replied scornfully, irritated by the man's behaviour. The man in the blue jacket rose slowly from his chair and withdrew bundles of wrinkled banknotes from his inside pocket. He handed them to Jogyo: '5,000 or nothing.' Hesitating briefly, Jogyo accepted the deal.

I had just been sold for the modest sum of 5,000 yuan.

At least he doesn't look like a violent man, I thought, slightly comforted.

The man who had just bought me looked at me and smiled, saying he owned a lot of land.

That's right, and I'm the one who's going to have to work your wretched land, you brute ...

His name was Seong-ho Kim and he was forty-six years old. He too was Chinese of Korean descent. On 22 April 1998 we said goodbye to Jogyo and I followed Seong-ho to the bus. We were now a couple. It was there, in the dusty bus station in Mudanjiang, that my youth came to an end.

He bought me a meal of rice and vegetables. He told me that we would take the bus to go to his place. When we got on the bus, he sat right behind me. The journey lasted almost three hours. The road was narrow and led through valleys with very steep hillsides. The landscape strangely resembled the one in North Korea that was familiar to me. As the bus twisted and turned, shaking all the while, I gripped the edge of the seat – I was afraid I would die without seeing my family again. Seong-ho didn't talk much. He was quiet, but I didn't trust him.

Night was falling when the bus finally came to a stop.

CHAPTER THIRTEEN

'Come on, follow me!' Seong-ho ordered as we got off the bus.

His house was located in a village at the foot of a mountain range that we could make out on the horizon. We had to walk to get there. It wasn't far from the Russian border. A dirt track led us alongside dense pine forests. It occurred to me that Seong-ho could kill me and no one would know – a thought that reawakened the fear muted by my exhaustion. Halfway there, Seong-ho stopped at a little restaurant by the side of the road and bought himself a pork dish for dinner. I supposed he would eat it when we arrived at his house; he didn't offer me any.

After twenty minutes of walking, we arrived at last in Rimku and stood before a small house with a thatched roof that reminded me of *Halmeoni's*. Despite the late hour, Seong-ho's parents were waiting for us. With them was another, younger couple: his brother and sister-in-law, who were staying over on their way somewhere. Seong-ho's mother, who had greying hair and the bent back of an old woman, wore an embittered expression and was cold and distant. His father was much warmer and even smiled when he saw me. He limped slightly and had trouble using his right arm.

We had barely finished with our introductions when Seong-ho, wishing to take me on a tour of my new home, led me to the kitchen, off which was a small bedroom: *our* bedroom. It was repulsive: the walls were dilapidated and the cement floor showed through the many holes in the greenish vinyl covering it. Using the toilet required going outside and crossing the courtyard to some sort of hut. Inside on the ground was a wooden board with a hole in it. Even though it was located a good distance from the bedroom, the hut gave off a stench of ammonia that filled the entire house – it was disgusting.

Once the tour was complete, Seong-ho's parents invited us to eat dinner. We sat around a low table. Seong-ho placed the pork dish he'd bought along the way in the middle of the table and sat down next to me.

'How did you get out alive?' his brother asked me, speaking with the accent of a *Chosun-jok*, or Chinese person of Korean descent. He wasn't speaking Chinese at all, but rather a Korean dialect that I could understand perfectly. He sat down across from us with a mocking air and placed his glass of rice wine on the table.

As they emptied glass after glass, the two brothers began to snigger. In fact, they didn't believe the stories about North Korea. To them, it was all a joke. The all-powerful Great Leader, the political oppression, the famine … no one in China was interested in any of it. Their father, Mr Kim, the only one who was polite, knew a little bit more about my country. In the 1960s, during the Cultural Revolution, he had fled to North Korea. He still remembered the delicious fish, especially the yellow pollack, that he ate while there and that made him feel nostalgic.

I gobbled down my bowl of rice without paying much attention to what was being said at the table. After so many years of deprivation I had a voracious appetite and nothing in the world could distract me from it. By the end of the meal, Seong-ho had had so much to drink that he could barely stand up. Gesturing with his hand in the direction of the bedroom, he indicated that I should follow him and mumbled that he was glad to have married me. He ordered me to lie down with him but I was too disgusted by the smell of alcohol. Terrified, I crouched in a corner of the room, my knees tucked up under my chin. I didn't move. After asking me a few more times, he finally fell asleep.

Around four in the morning, I heard someone shouting his name outside. I still hadn't dared to leave my safe corner. It was a friend of Seong-ho's who was waiting for him to go to work in the fields. But Seong-ho had drunk too much and was in no shape to get up.

'You go for me,' he mumbled. Then he started snoring again.

Almost relieved to be able to leave that room, I hurried outside.

'Welcome to China!' said his friend when he saw me.

This warm welcome was so unexpected I didn't even know what to say in response. There was goodness in his eyes. Seeing my awkwardness, he put me at ease by talking about himself. He had just done ten years of prison time for a crime he didn't commit and he was happy to be out; he was also happy to have married a Chinese woman who was about to give him a baby. Even here in the depths of Rimku, cut off from the rest of the world and experiencing a world of pain, I found a trace of human kindness. That gave me hope. The dismal experiences this man had gone through had not left him bitter; on the contrary, they enabled him to fully embrace people who were also suffering. Realising this comforted me – it made my solitude a little less unbearable.

Seong-ho, on the other hand, was not the type of person who is improved by misfortune. He had lived a loose life, gambling away his money and even stealing from his mother since he was a teenager. Desperate, she had come up with the idea of finding her eldest son, on whom she'd focused all her energy for his entire life, a wife in the hope that she would change him – that *I* would change him. She had more or less managed to tame him through high school, but once he became an adult she couldn't control him any more.

'I paid a lot of money for you – borrowed money to boot! You'd best do everything I say or I'll denounce you. I could even kill you and no one would notice!' she croaked at me from the kitchen when I came home from the fields, exhausted, that evening. She watched my every move like a hawk. I didn't react to her provocations, so she continued to talk to herself.

Truth be told, no one in the village liked her much. I found out later that they called her crazy and said I had every reason to be afraid of her. Even as I obeyed her every command, I avoided her as much as I could.

***

All the Chinese people of Korean descent in this village were monitoring me! I was the first North Korean to set foot there and the villagers came to the house to see the 'slave'. When they did, they threatened me, telling me they'd turn me in or kill me if I tried to escape. Poverty and misery make people do certain things and in this case had reduced these people to soulless creatures whose only instincts were hatred and wickedness.

Seong-ho spent his days drinking, smoking and gossiping with the neighbours. The reason he had bought me was becoming clearer and clearer: he didn't want to work in the cornfields any more. So now, after all my efforts in North Korea *not* to become a farmer, I found myself a field hand. I'd been uprooted from my native soil in the hope of finding a better life, only to become a slave.

A slave who didn't eat at the table with the others, who settled for rice and kimchi while the rest of the family ate meat and fish, who ploughed the fields during the day, cleaned the house and cooked dinner in the evening, and who had to submit to the demands of her husband at night.

A slave.

***

It didn't take long for me to get pregnant. It was early July and already hot. I didn't tell Seong-ho, but I did talk about it with Mrs Han, the village's union president. This was a rule: women had to notify her when they were pregnant. A forty-something Chinese woman of Korean descent, like the others, Mrs Han seemed kind. She suggested I have an abortion right away – the baby would have no civil status if it were born.

She's right, I can't keep this baby. I certainly wouldn't want to bring a child from that man into the world.

It turned out that it was a mistake to have told Mrs Han, because she told Seong-ho the very next day. A baby would mean one more mouth to feed. Seong-ho's mother said I should have an abortion at all costs. But no hospital would agree to do it because I didn't have papers. And even if one did, who would pay the bill? There was only one solution: a back-alley abortion.

Lost and alone, I didn't want a baby who would have to grow up in that squalid house. What would I eventually tell my child about our situation? That he was born to a mother without any legal status, that he could never go to school like other children nor work once he was grown. Desperately, I looked for answers to these questions. I would even have turned to *Unni* if she had been there. How I missed her – I didn't hold as a much of a grudge as before. Solitude had blunted my resentment.

It took me a very, very long time to get a hold of myself and see things more clearly, but the truth finally did surface, clear as day: an illegal abortion was out of the question. So I thought about the possibility of keeping the child. Little by little, an idea began to take shape. Every day it became a bit clearer. This child would stay neither in Rimku nor with this family. This child would give me hope. This child would save me by creating in me a space for happiness, even in the midst of misery. After a week, I'd taken my decision: we would go on this journey together. The union president, Mrs Han, turned a blind eye – she let me keep the baby.

Seong-ho was drinking more and more, while I continued to work in the rice paddies and cornfields, hiding my growing belly as best I could. His mother would use any excuse to deprive me of food, so I worked twice as hard in order to earn my evening bowl of rice: the baby and I could not afford to skip a meal.

One day Seong-ho's brother made a pass at me. I took the opportunity to suggest to my husband that we leave his parents' house and live somewhere else. We could set up our house in the little cottage at the top of the hill that Seong-ho's friend, the one with whom I worked in the fields, had helped me find. Other North Korean women before me had found safe haven there – the latest one had just left and the place was available.

To my surprise, Seong-ho agreed right away and we moved out a few days later. The house measured barely 4 square metres. There was just enough room for a mattress, two bowls and an electric heater. But it was our space – *my* space! Now I could work for myself instead of labouring as Seong-ho's replacement in exchange for a little rice and vegetables. I was terribly hungry, but I kept myself from eating too much because I wanted to set aside as much rice as possible for hard times to come.

One day an old Chinese woman, a former prostitute who lived in the area, took pity on me and gave me a bit of rice. Having been orphaned at a young age, she knew the pain of being abandoned and was very generous towards me.

'Look at what a state that witch of a mother-in-law has left you in! She could at least take care of you a little.'

I don't know why this woman showed me so much kindness. She reminded me of my mother and of *Unni*. I missed them so much in spite of their betrayal, which at the time I had considered unforgivable. Almost a year had passed since I had gone away. I had their phone number, but I couldn't call them: not only was there no phone at Seong-ho's house, but his family would not have wanted me to have any contact with the outside world. They were afraid I'd escape.

I was utterly alone.

***

On 20 April 1999, at 4am, I had my first contractions. In moments of pain and weakness, we ask for help even from our enemies: I made the mistake of waking Seong-ho.

'What's all this racket? Take your screaming outside! Now! Get outta here!' he told me.

But I was howling so loudly that the neighbours heard me, and they sent over a midwife before Seong-ho could throw me out. When she got there, she shook me hard and told me not to fall asleep because it could kill the baby. I was in labour for eleven hours, worn out by the time the baby came. It was a boy, and I named him Chul. The name means iron: strong as iron to face this pitiless world. Seeing his little face filled me with happiness. Chul the Sturdy … He was my child of hope, and from then on my only reason for living.

***

The baby's arrival did nothing to change Seong-ho's habits: he continued to drink just as much.

'We'll sell it!' he said when he came home one day. 'It'll help me pay off my debts.'

'I beg you, no – it's your firstborn child! You can't sell your first-born!'

Sobbing, I got on my knees to beg him. For the first time since bringing me to his house one year earlier, he seemed to hear me.

I was breastfeeding my baby but I didn't have enough milk. When the midwife found out I had given him a little sugar water, she railed against me, calling me clueless, telling me I could have killed my child. Seong-ho's father, Mr Kim, was the only person who gave any thought to my needs. He came to visit every now and then.

'How are you going to feed this child? You'll never make enough money selling rice cakes at the market,' he said, giving me some pig's feet bought with money he'd borrowed from a friend.

He was right, I couldn't make it alone. After careful consideration, I came up with the idea of asking Seong-ho to get in touch with my family and inform them of Chul's birth. He got all worked up, just as I'd predicted, but I kept pleading with him and eventually he relented. Seong-ho was not a cruel man at heart – at best he was spineless and lazy.

One afternoon well into the month of May, a few minutes after I'd returned from the market, there was a knock at the door: it was my sister and brother.

'*Unni*!!! Jeong-ho!!! What a surprise! Come in!' I cried, barely able to contain my excitement.

Seeing who it was, Seong-ho politely left us to ourselves: he had granted my wish.

It had only been two years since my siblings and I had seen each other, but we hugged with all the passion of people who had been separated for a lifetime, with the intensity of those who knew that this reunion might be their last. We dried our tears and I followed their haggard eyes as they gazed around the room. I didn't want their pity, but they had a hard time hiding their unease. After all, wasn't it their fault that I was forced to live in such a place? Before they could get a word in, I asked: 'Where's Mother?'

'She couldn't get away. She's in the throes of menopause and losing a lot of blood. You know how superstitious she is. She didn't want to enter the house of a newborn in her state,' *Unni* said.

'And Sang-chul?'

'He's well, too, doing this and that – working in the fields, repairing cars. All in all, he's managing pretty well.'

No sooner had she finished speaking than my sister withdrew from her bag a small square-shaped cloth bundle, which she handed to me. Inside were baby clothes my mother had set aside for me. They were far from new and they weren't pretty, but they brought tears to my eyes. I hugged the half-opened bundle to my chest and stood without moving so I could savour that moment of grace. This was a gift that could come only from a mother, for only a mother could understand the grand turmoil that a newborn can bring into a woman's life.

As though confirming my thoughts, Chul's cries interrupted the silence, bringing me back to reality.

I asked *Unni*: 'How much did that middleman give you after I was sold?'

'*Eomeoni* got … 1,000 yuan.'

'1,000?! What a joke! I was sold for *five*!'

Unni cringed.

Horrified, I tried in vain to contain my shock.

What a piece of scum, that Jogyo … I knew he would take a cut, but to keep 4,000 for himself … he should have given them at least three!

Sensing our discomfort, *Unni* resumed the conversation: 'Thanks to you, Sang-chul and I have our own house now.'

I couldn't believe my ears. I had been sold so that Unni *and Sang-chul could get a new house? And what about* Eomeoni *in all of this? Shouldn't you have used the money to take care of* Eomeoni*? You're despicable, the lot of you!*

'Please forgive me, *Noona*,' my brother said.

Jeong-ho understood my anguish. In asking for forgiveness, he was admitting to the crime in which he had been indirectly complicit. And he was also admitting that he had no explanation to offer.

At least he's asking for my forgiveness. But what about Unni*? Does she feel guilty at least?*

Unni set about frenetically cleaning the little house and folding the laundry. She would have done anything to avoid the weight of my gaze and doing domestic chores suited her to a tee. To keep our composure, Jeong-ho and I began to talk about our father. We wanted to believe that he was still alive, but we knew that it was most likely he had left us and that today another family lived in our flat.

When Jeong-ho asked me how I was doing, I had no answer for him. Of course, he could imagine what it was like for two people to live in 4 square metres deep in the heart of the Chinese countryside, but I didn't share with him that Seong-ho was also violent and that he beat me almost every day. I didn't tell him that when he lost at cards he would come home drunk and grab every object he could put his hands on and throw it against the wall and punch me in front of our child. I didn't want to share these details of my life – out of discretion, of course, but also because I didn't want him to feel guiltier about me than he already did.

Unni left the next morning but Jeong-ho stayed on for a few days. One evening after he'd been drinking, he told me why he'd left the army. Every soldier was obliged to remit money or make donations to the army on a regular basis, but in 1997 he hadn't been able to. During the months that preceded his desertion, he had tried his hand at trading gold, but it hadn't worked out. In October of that year, he and a few comrades were left without a choice: they had to flee.

'Kim Jong-Il,' I cried, 'that son-of-a-bitch!'

It was a cry that came straight from my heart. For once, I wasn't afraid of the consequences.

***

In January 2000, five other North Korean women and I were arrested by the Chinese police. Barely a year earlier, I had been the only one in the village, but in the months that followed many others had, like me, decided to seek survival on the other side of the Tumen River. These checks were routine, though, so I wasn't too worried.

A few yuan slipped under the table as usual, I told myself, *and everything will be fine*.

When we got to the station, one of the police officers asked with a mischievous grin, 'Do you know what happens to kids with Chinese fathers when they're sent back to North Korea?' He answered his own question while casually pouring himself some tea: 'They kill them! If I were you, I'd sell your son. You could get 10,000 yuan – twice the amount you'll have to pay us to get out of here.'

I still had not recovered from what the policeman had just said when Seong-ho arrived at the station, out of breath. They told him it would cost him 5,000 yuan to get me out of there. When the officer suggested selling our child, Seong-ho didn't hesitate to approve of the idea.

The world was collapsing before my eyes.

Three days went by with no solution. Chul and I were exhausted from waiting. The Chinese New Year was approaching, and on the fourth day the officers told me they were going to do me a favour and let me go in exchange for a written promise: that I would bring them 5,000 yuan after New Year.

This is a little gift, fallen from the sky, I said to myself. *Even in the depths of misery, there's always a glimmer of hope.*

But Seong-ho didn't have the 5,000 yuan in question and I couldn't reach my family to ask for help lest an unwise move on my part trigger their arrest. What was I to do? How was I going to manage? An idea came to me: to go and see Jogyo, the middleman who had sold me to Seong-ho in Mudanjiang. The man who had raped me. The man who had only given my mother 1,000 yuan. In spite of the horrific things he had subjected me to, he was the only person connecting me to the outside world, the only one I could turn to.

A few days later, while Seong-ho slept, I left the house with Chul at dawn.

The journey to Mudanjiang was shorter than I'd remembered. Chul was asleep on my back when I rang the bell of Jogyo's house. His wife answered, and her face froze when she saw my child. It was so obvious that I was in trouble that she had no choice but to invite me in. Jogyo would take me in for two days, but he couldn't advance me the money. He explained that the only solution was to get out of Rimku as soon as possible. As a North Korean without papers I couldn't rent a house, and he advised me to convince Seong-ho to escape to Mudanjiang with me: I needed him, if only to be able to rent a house.

***

On 19 April 2000, when Seong-ho, Chul and I had been in Mudanjiang for a few months, my sister Myeong-sil, her husband, Sang-chul, their daughter, Soo-jung, and my brother, Jeong-ho, appeared on our doorstep one morning. Everyone except Mother.

They needed a place to stay.

I let them in and set them up in the bedroom as best I could. Our mother had left the Chinese man, leaving them all homeless. Since arriving in China, Mum had still not succeeded in setting up a successful business, and on 18 March 2000 she had left them all to go to Shangdong, a city in southwest China where she would try her luck once again. *Eomeoni* had been such a canny businesswoman, so clever with her pig farming, the cigarettes and the seafood, yet in China she had failed. The news grieved me. Given *Unni's* evasive expression, I could tell she wasn't revealing everything and that I had every reason in the world to be worried. Might our mother have been sold off, like me? With whom was she living? Was she in good health? It was only much later that I learned that her life in China had been a tragedy right from the start.

As for me, I was living in a room scarcely big enough for two, earning 10 yuan a day by selling soy bean sprouts I grew at home: feeding four more mouths was going to be a challenge. My niece, Soo-jung, was my one source of joy. She was seven years old and played beautifully with Chul, her cousin who might never have been born. They would grow up together and keep each other company their whole lives. The idea of it made me happy enough to forget for a few days the trying, stressful situation we were in.

Sang-chul knew I wouldn't be able to house them indefinitely and that they would soon have to leave the village; he also knew that I was unhappy. He asked me to be patient: he was going to help me … once they got to South Korea.

'*South Korea?!*' I exclaimed, utterly dumbfounded. 'But that's enemy territory!'

'We've been preparing for the trip for two years now,' he said. 'One of my clients whose car I fixed gave me the idea. He's going to help us. We'll go to Dailan, in Liaodong Province, a two-hour drive from here. From there, we'll take the boat. Lots of North Koreans live in South Korea now, you know. You'll see – it'll all work out!'

Typical of him to be so enthusiastic! I know that fake confidence too well. Didn't we give ourselves over to his certitude two years ago when he got us all to come to China? At the end of the day, isn't it because of him that we abandoned our father – and our fatherland?

'Come with us! It won't be an easy journey, but I just know this will work.'

'I can't. I'm too afraid of Seong-ho. I have to stay in China.'

After a long debate, we came to an agreement: I would go find Mother, and together, she, my son and I would catch up with them.

***

Three weeks after they arrived in Mudanjiang, *Unni*'s family and my brother left for Dailan. They didn't want to go without me, but I was firm about staying. I refused to put my fate in other people's hands again – I had paid dearly enough for it the first time.

As soon as they arrived in South Korea, Sang-chul promised, they would send me money. Jeong-ho was trying to act like someone who was going away on holiday, but he was terrible at hiding his anxiety.

'I'll buy you lots of toys when I get to South Korea, Chul,' he said, hugging my son. 'Meanwhile, take good care of your mum.'

On 19 April 2000, we had breakfast together: Chinese bread, milk and beans. Then it was time to leave. As they waved goodbye, my family gestured to me not to stand too long in the doorway.

We didn't know it then, but that was the last breakfast we would ever have together.

I spent the days following their departure waiting for a sign of life, wondering if they'd arrived at their destination. One night, my brother came to me in a dream: *Jeong-ho, don't go that way, that road leads to North Korea. Come back!*

I woke up in a sweat and told my dream to Seong-ho, who was lying next to me.

'Makes perfect sense to me. I knew they'd never make it,' he said coldly.

I tried to go back to sleep, but my heart was heavy.

CHAPTER THIRTEEN

The next afternoon, there was a knock at the door: it was the man who had helped Sang-chul organise their escape. My heart raced as I invited him inside.

'Sang-chul and Jeong-ho were arrested,' he told me.

My heart stopped.

'What about *Unni*?' I stammered, barely able to breathe. 'Where is *Unni*?'

'Your sister sure is lucky. The policeman took pity on her kid, he let the two of them go.'

Every day after that, I waited for *Unni*. I thought she'd come back to me right away. More than once I had the chance to leave Seong-ho and flee, but I wanted to wait for *Unni* and Soo-jung. I kept delaying my escape but it was no use: I never saw her again.

***

Three years passed without news of my family: nothing from *Eomeoni*, *Unni*, her husband or Jeong-ho. Living with the constant fear that I would be denounced and lose Chul, I became increasingly isolated and lonely. When I learned that the market in Mudanjiang where I sold my bean sprouts was to close, Chul was four. He had grown a lot. I was amazed that he was able to speak both Korean and Chinese fluently.

How would we earn a living without that market? How would we pay the rent? It wasn't as if Seong-ho was going to take care of things after all these years of doing absolutely nothing! I was searching desperately for a solution when I heard a rumour: a new market was opening in Harbin, the capital of Heilongjiang Province and home to three and a half million people. In Chinese, the word for 'crisis' consists of two characters: danger and opportunity. Harbin was a huge city, one that would give me anonymity. This was my opportunity, this was my future.

In March 2003, Seong-ho, Chul and I left Mudanjiang for Harbin.

CHAPTER FOURTEEN

Another day without selling a thing. I knew when I came to Harbin that this old market outside the city didn't get a lot of traffic, but I couldn't have imagined it would be this deserted. Paralysed by cold and fatigue, my feet aching, I wrapped up my red chilli powder, turnips and dried seaweed and began to break down my stand. I looked around; I was one of the few people who always hung around until evening in hopes of picking up some half-price vegetables that hadn't sold that day. What dish would I prepare that night? When you don't have much to eat, all you think about is food. My eyes spied a bunch of chives on the table of the vendor next to me. That was it: tonight, I would make a chive omelette, Chul's favourite. I took a handful of chives and stuffed them in my bag before heading to the babysitter's to get my son.

Heilongjiang Province is known for its endless winters and the year 2004 was no exception. The wind was whipping my cheeks, so I walked quickly. Luckily, the babysitter's apartment was on my way home. Harbin, the capital of Heilongjiang, had a population of 3.5 million and the city teemed with people and tall buildings and dazzling neon lights. Moving here a few months earlier had given me what I needed most since coming to China in 1998: anonymity. I had tamed my terror of the unknown and made it my accomplice. Now, with my fake papers, I passed for a Chinese citizen of Korean descent. No one suspected I was North Korean – it was perfect.

The family who took care of Chul for 25 yuan a month in their home also cared for seven other children. This arrangement served me well: they didn't ask any questions about who we were, and they kept my son all day while I sold vegetables at the market. Only five years old then, Chul didn't know how to tell the time, but he was always right there in front of his babysitter's place, with his blue sweater and his good humour, at five on the dot.

'*Umma! Umma*'s here! My *umma*'s here!' he'd cry out in Korean as soon as he saw me. Then he'd run to me and hold me tight.

I loved to feel the warmth of his small body next to mine, to hold his hand on the walk home. It reminded me of *Halmeoni* and how she used to hold me in her arms when I lived with her in Pukchong. My parents had never walked me to school – their days were too full, they didn't have time to look after children. I wondered who the real loser was: I, who had wanted for affection, or my parents, who had never learned to give it?

Once home, I put Chul in the main room and headed to the kitchen to prepare dinner. I could see him as I sautéed the chives. He was playing silently by himself in a corner of the room, making paper aeroplanes. In another corner was Seong-ho, who came home blind-drunk every day. I would try to teach Chul some maths before dinner, but he had trouble concentrating – he was tired from coughing all day. When he was barely a month old he had developed a high fever, and at eleven months he'd got pneumonia, which had weakened his lungs. He'd had a constant cough ever since but I couldn't even consult a doctor, since taking him to hospital meant risking being reported to the police. The only medicine I could get was Zhitongpian, an adult-strength pain reliever used, among other things, to ease menstrual cramps. It was very strong and I knew it wasn't good for him, but it was the only medicine I could put my hands on at the market – the medicine sold in pharmacies was just too expensive.

Chul's illness had eliminated his appetite, so he rarely finished his meals, but that evening, thanks to the eggs and chives, he managed to eat his whole bowl of rice. Getting him to swallow a dose of the bitter Zhitongpian was another matter, but I went about it with patience and persistence. Once the mealtime was over, I began to get ready for the next day. I set the *doraji*, or bellflower roots, to soak so my customers could buy them ready to eat. The process was somewhat painstaking. In order to be preserved, bellflower roots must first be dried in the sun. The day before selling them, I'd soak them in water to refresh them. Then all I had to do was add a little soy sauce, sesame oil and garlic, and hey presto, they were ready to be eaten as a *banchan*, or side dish, along with some rice.

It was already 9pm when I began grinding more dried red chilli peppers. This was usually the time when I could feel the angst rising in me. I hadn't known a single peaceful night since coming to China. The silence amplified the least little sound, leaving me wide awake for the rest of the night. Seong-ho, drunk, was now soundly asleep. I consoled myself with the thought that at least tonight we'd be spared his violent fits of anger. Chul had always been terrified of his father. I'd thought of leaving Seong-ho more than once, but that was impossible: he knew where my mother and sister were staying, and if I escaped he'd report them immediately to the police. Six years earlier, I had abandoned my father by leaving North Korea. He had begged me to save my brother, but there too I had failed. There was no way I was going to allow this man to put my mother and sister in harm's way. One day they would come for me, I just knew it.

That night, 21 April 2004, around 10pm, I was curled up with Chul as usual. He had got into a bad habit of refusing to go to bed alone and I would lie next to him until he dozed off, gently patting his back to lull him to sleep. I never did tell him stories the way *Halmeoni* did back in Pukchong when I was his age, I was just too tired after the long days at the market.

That's when I heard a muffled sound: it came from the front door. As I spun my head towards the window, I knew someone was there. I stayed next to Chul without moving so as not to wake him up, but the sound kept coming. I gently placed my hand over his mouth and lay there, motionless, in the dark. My senses were on high alert. I didn't know what to do, so I got up, went to the window and lifted a corner of the curtain. That's when I saw two faces pressed against the glass, peering into the room. I let go of the curtain and backed away towards my son, panicked as a falcon caught in a trap.

Bam bam bam!

'Open up!'

My heart stopped, my head spun. Who could it be? I didn't know anyone in the city. It could only be the police. Sensing danger, Chul threw himself into my arms and began to sob. Holding him tight, I motioned for him not to make a sound. Then I slumped to the ground, curled myself up in a ball and threw my arms over my head, as if by becoming as small as possible I might disappear. My son's cries brought me back to reality. Without stumbling over a single word in Chinese, I calmly said,

'Who's there? It's late. What are you doing here at this hour?'

'Open the door,' a man's voice ordered.

His cool, authoritative tone threw me into more of a panic. My forehead was dripping with cold sweat. I took a deep breath to slow my heartbeat and calm my nerves, then I opened the door.

There in front of me stood about ten men in uniform. *This is it,* I thought, *the moment I've dreaded so long, the moment of my arrest.* They all stared at me, stone-faced, as if ready to pounce on their prey. I searched for words, praying some would find their way from my throat to my mouth, but none came. Seconds later, one of the officers grabbed my arm and handcuffed me. I hadn't known chains could be so heavy. The weight of the chain that bound my wrists threw off my centre of gravity, forcing me to lean forward. From this awkward position I experienced the rest of my apprehension as it unfolded: walking out the door, hearing the screams of my son and the voices of the policemen, the general commotion. No one came to our aid. All our neighbours were Chinese – it wouldn't have been like them to lift a finger to help, not even to prevent a murder.

In fact, the only Chinese person to be disturbed by what was happening was Seong-ho.

'Quiet!' he growled from the far end of the room, his voice gravelly. 'Shut the hell up!'

He was so drunk and sluggish he could barely open an eye. He got up clumsily from his mat. It was as though he hadn't even noticed the presence of the policemen in the room.

'*Gannashiki* ... *gannashiki* ... you whore,' he kept muttering.

An officer asked to see his papers but he didn't have any. Unable to get his life together, he'd lived without an ID for the past ten years.

The other officers had already escorted me outside when my son and his father came out, one after the other. The police put me in a car parked in front of the house and had Chul and Seong-ho get in another vehicle parked behind it. My son's cries were swallowed up by the silence of the frozen night. Soon, I could hear only the sound of the car engine. I stole a look at my watch: it was a little after 10pm. Wedged between two burly officers in the back seat, I could scarcely breathe. Then they blindfolded me.

'Head down!' they ordered, pushing my forehead to my knees. I was a criminal and criminals don't get to look around. I tried to stay calm, but I was worried about Chul. How were they treating him in the other car? In mine, the officers were chattering calmly. They talked about what they'd had for dinner that evening, even exchanged a couple of jokes. It was as though I didn't exist. I felt so small. Smaller than the bit of dried radish I'd been preparing for the next day's market barely an hour before.

The car ride was starting to feel long, and I realised we weren't headed for the local police station. Fear gripped me. My stomach was in knots. At long last, the car stopped and the men led me out, my head still lowered. As I still couldn't see anything, I let myself be guided. I crossed what seemed like a threshold into a building, then went through another doorway. At last they took off my blindfold and allowed me to raise my head and sit down. We were in a small, bare room lit by a single naked bulb hanging from the ceiling. There were two desks, two chairs and a stool. The walls were white, but they seemed black to me. The policemen sat at their desks and began filling out forms. As I sat on the stool, facing them, I looked around frantically for Chul but didn't see him. Suddenly it occurred to me that I might never see him again. Taken away by the police, handcuffs binding my wrists – was that the last image my son would have of his mother? Over and over, I asked where he was, but they just told me to wait.

To make myself feel better, I told myself he must be with Seong-ho while they worked out the problem of his ID papers.

The policemen spoke to me in Chinese and I answered in their language. I told them I was Chinese. One of them asked for my ID card. I always carried it in my pocket, even at night. Calmly, I held it out to him. The older one, who was around forty and rather chubby, placed his forefinger on the laminated card and looked right at me.

'I've seen a lot of fake ID cards in my time, but this one here is bloody worthless!'

No need to tell me. I knew full well it was a cheap imitation – I didn't have the 50 yuan it would take to get a quality fake. Acting as though nothing were wrong, I kept telling them that the card was real and I was the person on it: Yeongmi Park, Chinese citizen since 2003. That's when one of the men gave me a sheet of paper and told me to write my name, age, address, school and place of birth – in Chinese, of course.

I wasn't scared; I knew my written Chinese was good. I'd studied it in school ever since teaching Chinese had become mandatory, in the 1980s. Hangul, the Korean alphabet, had been invented by King Sejong in 1443, but Koreans had continued to write in Chinese because it was the official language of historical documents. At school I'd also been taught that South Koreans were very good at Chinese and that if we wanted control of the peninsula after reunification, we'd have to measure up.

This was the moment of truth. Would all those hours I'd spent bent over my school desk finally pay off? Very carefully I wrote that

I was born in Jilin and that my parents were Man-soo Park and Gum-hee Lee.

The officers were surprised to see I knew so many characters.

'We're from the Ministry of Foreign Affairs,' said the one who had scrutinised my ID card.

At least they're not the police, I thought. Officials from the Ministry of Foreign Affairs didn't go around arresting people just like that. This was sort of good news.

'Your Chinese is very good, almost better than mine!'

Taking the sheet of paper I'd just written on, the two men left the room. I knew they were deciding my fate. Would they let me go? They might also demand a bribe. How much would they ask for? And where would I get the money? They could just as easily send me to prison. Put a ring through my nose, like a cow. People would point at me, I'd be a laughingstock. And who would take care of Chul? Wasn't it enough that I had abandoned my father six years ago? Did I now have to abandon my son? I was weary, so very tired. The wait seemed endless.

Finally, the two men came back.

'Where is my son?' I asked them.

'He's in the room next door. You'll see him in a minute,' said one of the men. Then he calmly added, 'You know, you could've passed for Chinese, but the person who reported you told us you're North Korean. She didn't just call the local police station, either – she called the Ministry. I'm afraid we have to send you back to North Korea.'

He looked hard at me with a mocking expression.

'You know you can always come back. Go ahead and try it, you'll see!'

No! This couldn't be happening. What about Chul? He mustn't come to North Korea with me, he would die of hunger. He absolutely had to remain in China. I'd seen too many children perish and too many made into orphans. I didn't want want my son to turn out like Mrs Jang's son, swollen and pale … If Chul stayed in China,

Seong-ho could take him to my mother and sister's place and they would take care of him.

All these thoughts were racing through my mind, but I mustn't show it.

'What about my son?' I asked coolly, my voice calm. '*He* was born in China.'

'You can leave him here or take him with you. It's up to you.'

I was instantly relieved but the relief didn't last long, for my next thought was that if Chul and I were separated, I might never see him again. Tears filled my eyes and ran down my cheeks. I had never in my life felt such despair – not even foraging for roots on Mount Nangpo in hopes of finding something to put in my belly.

Tears blurred my vision, but I looked at my watch: four in the morning. Once again, I was handcuffed and blindfolded. Once again, the officers pushed my head down and led me to the waiting car outside. *This is it*, I said to myself. *I'm done for, they're taking me to prison.* As soon as the men and I were in the back seat, the driver set off. It was a long ride. I had only one desire: to see Chul one more time before I was sent back to China. It was still dark when we arrived at Harbin Prison. Surrounded by a perimeter wall and barbed wire, it was a terrible-looking place. The gate was open; they were expecting us. The first guard wore a vacant expression and a uniform of yellowish beige. He checked our papers and we crossed the courtyard to the main entrance, a large wire-mesh door that led inside the prison building. I was taken to the toilet and then to a changing room, where I was told to put on an iron-grey uniform.

I stood there, frozen in place, as though my feet had sunk into the cement. Before me stretched a dimly lit corridor lined on both sides by the wire-mesh doors of the cells. Complete silence, not a prisoner in sight. The guard motioned me towards the first open door. I followed him down the long corridor as he jangled his big set of keys. At the very end, we stopped in front of a cell – *my cell.* It was windowless and narrow. The smell of mould blending with the stench of sweat and excrement almost made me vomit. The sullen-looking guard approached and, with a jerk of his chin, indicated I should go in. The door closed behind me, like a verdict.

In the shadowy half-light I could just make out a woman asleep on the floor. There was a pile of folded blankets in one corner, but no sleeping mats. When the woman woke, she treated me with utter indifference. She rose and went to take the bowl of broth that had been pushed through the flap at the base of the door. About twenty years old, she had long hair. Her expression was so bleak and her body so scrawny it looked like blood no longer flowed through her veins.

So began my first stay in prison. I didn't know then that there would be many others.

I spent the following day sitting on the floor, alone. My cellmate disappeared in the morning without a word and didn't return until evening. I didn't know where she went, so when she came back I asked her. She told me that all the inmates worked on construction sites during the day. She was a practitioner of Falun Gong, the religion banned by the Chinese government, and her parents had reported her to the police. During her first six months in prison, her parents hadn't visited and she thought she'd die of hunger. The broth and hunk of bread the prison served each morning weren't enough to live on; an inmate's family members or friends had to bring dinner to the prison. Then one day, my cellmate's father came to visit and made her promise not to follow Falun Gong any more. She promised, and her family began to visit her. She only had twelve months left to serve. Unlike me, she had parents and a home to go back to once she left prison. I was terribly jealous.

As for me, I had no visitors, so I didn't eat though I gladly accepted my cellmate's scraps when she couldn't finish a meal. No one was waiting for me in North Korea. As far as my fellow countrymen were concerned, I was a traitor who had abandoned her homeland. In my own eyes I was something much worse: a mother who had abandoned her child in a foreign land.

I was so tired I couldn't even get up, let alone console myself. I longed to see Chul. Was he still alive? What would become of him if I left China? In one corner of the cell there was a toilet with no lid and a spigot above it. The surveillance camera, which was on twenty-four hours a day, did not reach that part of the cell, and I would hide out there and silently weep where the Chinese guards could not see me – I didn't want them to see my weakness. When they couldn't find me on the monitor, they'd come bang on the door. If I didn't answer, they'd open up and tell me to sit somewhere else.

On the third day, I couldn't take it any more. I jumped to my feet as though possessed by demons and began screaming and pounding on the door:

'Open up! Open up! I beg you!'

I had to act fast before leaving China. I ranted and raved and hit myself all over, but no one responded. After half an hour I collapsed to the floor, at my wits' end, my eyes red and my face soaked with tears. Hearing the racket, one of the inmates on my floor called to the guards:

'Who is that? What's she in for?'

'A North Korean. She'll be sent back soon,' one of the guards answered irritably.

'*Bei Chaoxian! Bei Chaoxian!* North Korean! North Korean!' The prisoners began to shout.

In their eyes, I was a freak, an anomaly. From that day on, I became known as 'the Korean spy'.

***

Three days later, completely out of the blue, I heard a voice in the corridor. It couldn't be! I recognised that voice!

'*... ma ... ma!*'

I pounded on the door with my fists as hard as I could. In Korean, I shouted: '*Umma* is here, Chul! I'm right here!'

No answer. In the corridor, footsteps and voices. Then silence. A few minutes later, a key in the lock. The guard entered to hand me a parcel, but he was invisible to me. I lunged past him towards the door and ran barefoot down the hall, crying, 'Chul! Chul!' The guard caught me right away and brought me back to the cell.

'But I must see him! I must see him!' I cried as I struggled against him.

Chul had come this far … I'd been this close to taking him in my arms. It *had* to be his voice that I'd heard. I let out a harrowing scream that echoed all down the hall. Fury rose in me until the blood boiled in my brain. I was capable of killing someone. I absolutely had to talk to my son. I needed to tell him, *Umma will come back alive. Until then, you must stay healthy*. The words crashed around in my head, but I knew Chul could probably not hear them.

As though to calm me down, the guard held out a black plastic bag. Swallowing hard, he told me he had called my husband and asked him to bring clothes and money to pay for my meals. He had tried to arrange a meeting with my son and husband, but his superior officer had objected, so he'd had to send them back. But he did promise Chul to give me the bag he had brought his mum. 'These are *Umma's* favourite clothes. Please give them to her,' he'd said. These were the words Chul had left me with, the only trace of my son I could cling to.

Words that still resonate today.

I opened the black plastic bag: inside were a black jacket with a white collar and a pair of white trainers. We'd bought them together at the market a few years back. I had never worn them, I'd been saving them for a special occasion. Drying my tears, I silently thanked my son.

During the days that followed, once my cellmate left, the tiny cell turned into an enormous hell. In the end, the security camera that watched me twenty-four hours a day broke me. It became my friend.

'I want to speak to Chul,' I said to it over and over.

I stopped brushing my hair, I stopped sleeping. I spent my days seated on the floor of the cell, feeling like I was going mad. At the end of the sixth day, one of the older guards took pity and allowed me to come out into the corridor to get some air. I stood up and stepped out of the cell. Once again, I looked down the long, poorly lit corridor. To my left, two metal screens separated me from the guards' station. My cell was the first of many narrow cells crammed next to each other the length of the hallway. I only vaguely remembered the scene from when I had first arrived in the prison, not even a week earlier.

The guard knew I hadn't eaten and offered to order some food for me.

'What would you like? What do you feel like eating?'

In truth, I wasn't hungry. I couldn't account for it. The only dish that came to mind was corn broth, which reminded me of my mother. It also had been the only dish I could afford when I worked at the market in Harbin.

'Corn broth,' I mumbled.

'She could have asked me for anything, but she wants corn broth,' he said, gently mocking me. 'Corn broth it is.'

He promised to order that for me for the next day's breakfast and dinner.

'You have to eat if you want to come back to China and collect your son,' he added.

This wasn't exactly a revelation, but his words did comfort me. I came to my senses and asked him for a floor cloth – I'd lose my mind if I continued to do nothing. I washed that hallway floor furiously, as though it were my own skin I was cleaning, my skin that for so long had accumulated layer upon layer of filth. The floor shone. It was as clean as the floor of our housing block in Ranam, the one my mother washed so vigorously. Radiant as The Portrait my parents dusted every day, dazzling as our Beloved Father's smile, resplendent as Our Sun. Such thoughts led me back to Korea. Clearly, crying or begging not to be deported were pointless – I had to get used to the idea of going back.

Just then, I was overcome by the memory of my father. He would not be pleased to see me dressed in rags when I came to visit his grave. So I set about washing my trainers, cleaning them with toothpaste, working them over again and again until they were bright white, without a trace of filth. Maybe my body reeked from not having bathed in so long, but at least my shoes were spotless. (The water pressure was so low I couldn't take a shower – opening the tap produced no more than a dribble.) There wasn't enough room in my cell to dry my shoes and undergarments, but I kept on cleaning them, driven by the same fury with which I'd mopped the corridor. To raise my spirits, I told myself over and over, *The sooner I go back to Korea the better. I'll finally be able to visit* Abeoji's *grave.*

Early one afternoon a week later – the last day of April – the door opened and some officers entered my cell. I recognised the face of the officer who had interrogated me in his office in Harbin. They told me to gather my things. I put on the trainers I'd so carefully cleaned and grabbed my black plastic bag. It was all I had. Once again, I was handcuffed, blindfolded, and taken away in their car.

***

When I removed the blindfold, the clock of the train station said it was just after three in the afternoon. I recognised Harbin Station. It was covered in advertisements; the golden arches of McDonald's dominated the front of the building. You could pick out the workers by their grey and black garments – most likely they were coming back from a construction site – and the large sacks in which they had to carry around their own bedding, since the hotels in Harbin were not very well equipped. There were also children and women, and *chosun-jok*, as the locals called Chinese people of Korean descent. The women, all wearing make-up, were on their way to work in restaurants, karaoke bars and massage parlours.

Still standing in front of the station, I watched these people pass before me as if in a dream. Then a crowd began to form around me, as though the entire station had decided to gather right there and then. The officer standing beside me told the crowd I was North Korean and about to be sent home.

'Oh my God, she's off to North Korea …'

'Why is she wearing handcuffs?'

'She probably killed someone!'

There were whispers and murmurs but no one spoke to me directly. I heard 'That poor girl!' but also 'Get out of China!' I was the laughingstock of the crowd. The police officers had placed me smack bang in the middle of the square as if I were a side show and then stood watching me from the sidelines – they knew I couldn't do anything. Inside the train station, there were too many people and too much commotion for them to safely to leave their prisoner standing around, but in the middle of the square there was no risk of losing me. Mortified, I kept my head down and waited.

Two hours later, the train arrived at last and I was taken to a sleeping compartment. The two officers settled into the lower berths and I took the upper one. I lay there with my wrists cuffed to the bars of the bed, my face almost touching the ceiling. The berth was higher than the window, so I couldn't even look out at the night. I could hear the men drinking beer. At first, I was glad not to have to look anyone in the eye, but the relief was short-lived: having to use the toilet while handcuffed and with the door standing open was truly humiliating but I'd endured so many indignities by now I no longer knew which one was the worst.

I knew the train was approaching the tunnel that would lead us to Tumen, a border town separating China from North Korea. The prison there had been specially designed for North Koreans who had defected to China. It was my next destination. A week-long stay in Tumen Prison was a required step before you could enter the land of the 'Comrade Generalissimo Kim Jong-Il'.

CHAPTER FIFTEEN

The prison in Tumen was four storeys high; the building was brand new.

I know Chinese prisons. This doesn't scare me. Everything's going to be fine. I'll get back to North Korea soon, I told myself.

I grasped at any glimmer of hope: an image of my homeland welcoming me back with open arms warmed my heart – for a few seconds. But as soon as I entered the prison and was left in the interview room with a guard, a chubby man of about thirty, I had to clench my jaws to try to contain my anxiety, which had resurfaced despite my good attitude going into this. I asked that a female police officer perform the body search.

'*Gannashiki!* You whore! You'll do as you're told to do!' spat the guard as he gave me a hard kick in the shin.

With his pudgy hand he began to search me in places I normally keep hidden from others. He was looking for medicine or money, which female prisoners often hid inside themselves for survival. All of the female prisoners underwent this humiliating search before ending up behind bars.

***

To my astonishment, I found myself one of about forty North Korean women aged between ten and seventy, as well as about fifteen men. The women were divided among three cells and the men occupied a fourth. Not a single Chinese person, only North Koreans. Like me, they had been denounced and were waiting to be taken back to North Korea – I hadn't dreamt there would be so many of them.

Within the prison walls, conversations were a blend of brief, muffled, choppy whispers, but honest enough to create a real sense of solidarity. We were all fugitives with a shared destination: North Korea. One of the female prisoners was a graduate of Pyongyang University and had taught languages in China. Others were businesswomen like my mother. Some had already been sent back two or three times before ending up here again and waiting for the police to decide their fate.

One of the friendliest women told me there were spies everywhere and that I must be careful about what I told the guards. If I wanted to hide an object, the best thing to do was to swallow it. Thinking back to the search I'd endured when I arrived, I didn't hesitate to take her advice.

On average, people stayed in the Tumen prison about a week, but some had been there for six months or even a year. My stint lasted two weeks. Around the middle of May 2004, I returned at last to Korea.

***

That day, I was among the four women and four men who walked across the bridge linking the Chinese city of Tumen to the North Korean border town of Namyang. On the Chinese side of the bridge the policemen removed our handcuffs and handed us over to the North Korean officers. The first order our compatriots gave us was odd: we must remove our shoelaces so they could tie our wrists together. This was their version of handcuffs.

It said a lot about my country's economic situation. I was ashamed.

We were then driven by truck to Onsung, where the *Bowibu*, or state police agents, were waiting to interrogate us. Depending on the severity of our crimes, we would be sent to one of several different kinds of prison: Correction Camp (교화소), Political Prisoner Camp (정치범 수용소), Forced Labour Camp (노동 단련대) or Absolute Control Camp (완전 통제 구역). Watching an international television show was a political crime, for example, and the accused, along with his or her family, would be sent to Political Prisoner Camp for life.

Fortunately, my crime had been classified as 'economic' rather than 'political' so towards the end of May 2004, after being detained in the Onsung Prison for three weeks, I was sent to the Detention Centre (도 직결소) in Chongjin, where I was born. The Centre was located under the Ipche bridge, in the neighbourhood of Songpyeong. The bridge had been built in the 1980s and people called it Ipche, or 'stand out', because its unusual architectural design made it stand out from all the other bridges in the region.

I knew this Detention Centre, I knew it well. When I was eight years old, I would walk past it without stopping, terrified by the grey-uniformed prisoners who made bricks there. I'd speed up in front of the blue metal gates lest I make eye contact with a guard. Even though I was first in my class, every though I knew our country's history by heart as well as the birthdays of our leaders and the New Year's speeches by heart, I was overwhelmed with fear.

Now, twenty-eight years later, wearing that same grey uniform, I had gone through those blue metal gates.

***

At the Detention Centre, our days began at half-past four in the morning and ended at 11pm. All day long I dragged a plough full of fertiliser over dry, cracked dirt. I had no shoes and the sharp-edged stones that filled the dirt flayed my feet. The endless days repeated themselves over and over; we did not have a single day of rest.

In the evening, some women were called on to perform a different kind of work. Two guards would summon them into the kitchen. The women would not come out until the next morning. Generally speaking, those who had spent the night in the kitchen had less work to do the next day. Thankfully, I was never chosen – I would not have been able to make it through the horror of a second unwanted pregnancy.

One day in August 2004, I stepped on a piece of broken glass and cut my left foot. The guards forbade us from wearing shoes to discourage escape attempts and wounds on the bottom of our feet were common.

What I thought was a small scar from the cut turned a peculiar greenish hue and several days later I woke to find my leg so swollen I couldn't even take off my trousers – let alone stand up and walk. Over time my leg became darker and darker, until it was almost black. The guards told me I was going to die soon, that I had a one-in-two chance of surviving. They dispatched me immediately to the main Detention Centre in Chongjin because they didn't want a death on the books.

On 14 August 2004, the guards took me to the health clinic in Namchongjin. I recognised the place: it was where *Unni* had given birth to Soo-jung. The doctor examined my leg and recommended amputation. There was a way to treat it, but it would cost money. Knowing I didn't have any, he'd eliminated the second scenario from the outset. The guards decided I was worthless, clearly incapable of pulling a plough, and decided to drop me at the local police station. Thanks to my stubbornness, no one touched my leg and, on 20 August, the wife of *Jaguen Abeoji*, my aunt Eun-hee, whom the police had managed to contact, came and signed some papers.

I was free.

'I never want to see you again! Don't you ever set foot in our house!' my aunt hissed angrily as soon as we'd left the station.

'How is *Jaguen Abeoji*? How are the children? Can you give me any news?' I asked.

But she turned her back on me and started to walk away without answering.

'Can you at least tell me where to find my father's grave?' I persisted.

What had I just said? Turning around abruptly, she scowled at me, saying, 'You're nothing but a filthy, selfish person who only worries about her conscience! You want to visit your father's grave and pay your respects just to say you've done your daughterly duty. To have a clear conscience. Meanwhile, we've lost status because of you and your fine family. You think we have the luxury of tending to our conscience, of paying respects? Do you want to kill us? Disgusting, selfish person! Get out of here, I never want to see you again!'

Tears poured down my cheeks as I sank to the pavement. Tears of sadness and despair. My leg, covered in black pus, had held up this far, but now I felt it was going to fail me, to give me a good excuse to take the time to weep, to reach deep down inside myself in hopes of finding the strength I needed to get up again. Aunt Eun-hee wanted nothing more to do with me. She was protecting her family, I understood that – I would surely have done the same thing in her place. And yet I wanted so badly to tell *Jaguen Abeoji* the truth about the North Korean regime. I wanted to tell them both they'd been victims of brainwashing their entire lives, that there was another world out there, just over the border. I wanted to urge them to take their destiny into their own hands. I had learned, but they still lived with illusions.

I so wanted to tell them.

Not knowing where else to go, I let my feet lead me to my old flat, the one in which I'd abandoned *Abeoji* six years earlier. Maybe I would find a key under the kimchi pot. When I entered the foyer, I saw the door of the delegate of the block of flats open slightly. In the crack I could just make out a silhouette: it was Eun-joo *Umma*, the one who used to post poems by Kim Il-sung in the foyer and tell me to memorise them. That was in 1992 – a dozen years ago.

She had aged a lot. After quickly asking me about my family, she then disappeared behind her door. It was a fleeting encounter.

CHAPTER FIFTEEN

What is happening to us? Why am I treated so poorly in my own country? Why are people so indifferent? What has happened to the city I grew up in? I don't recognise it any more …

I wouldn't have had the courage to knock on her door, but Eun-joo *Umma* opened it again a few hours later. It was after midnight when she invited me in. The flat had not changed. As she helped me get settled in the bedroom, she explained that she could not be friendlier earlier for fear that she be seen by the neighbours. I told her about our journey into China, but I didn't dare ask for news of Father. She seemed to understand my pain and didn't go there. Instead, she surprised me with a totally unexpected bit of news:

'Your brother-in-law is alive.'

'Sang-chul? He's alive? What about Jeong-ho? Tell me everything, please!'

'I don't know anything about your brother, but Sang-chul was sent to a Forced Labour Camp and fell gravely ill. I think he's out now, that's all I know.'

As she stuck slices of raw potato to my leg – which she called anti-bacterial compresses – I swore to myself I would not try to contact them. Not Jeong-ho, not Sang-chul. It would be too dangerous for them. Eun-joo *Umma* woke me up at dawn the next morning and told me I had to leave the flat before daybreak. She slipped me a 20 yuan bill, wished me good luck and closed the door.

It was then, as I left her, that I suddenly felt devastatingly alone. I was in my birthplace, but now I had no one. The only person who might have been able to help me was my Aunt *Gomo*, but she lived in another city, and without papers it would have been impossible for me to get a travel permit to go and see her. I'd returned to my country and was no longer an illegal immigrant, but my status was now much worse: I was a criminal, an outlaw, someone whose mere presence put others in danger. I was unwanted. An outsider.

My leg was so swollen now that I could barely feel it, but somehow I managed to do what all homeless people do when they can't stay on the street: I headed for the train station.

It took me two hours to reach Chongjin station. A handsome granite building, it had been built in the 1950s and had high windows and a huge photo of Kim Il-sung above the entrance. Banners hung on either side of the portrait:

'Long live Comrade Kim Il-sung'
'Long live the glorious Workers Party'

These slogans which I had recited so adoringly when I was young made me profoundly sick that day.

In a corner of the station I saw some women selling biscuits, others bread, noodles or sweets. There were many people on the platform waiting impatiently, but it seemed the train would never arrive. There were merchants, too, and I could see from a distance that each carried two or three backpacks full of Chinese clothing and shoes, just as *Eomeoni* used to do. I also saw corpses lying on the platform among the travellers and merchants until guards or ticket sellers came to pile them up in a corner of the station. When the corpses were stacked more than ten high, they'd be taken outside and thrown into a truck.

I might have been one of them. When people saw my leg, they were so disgusted they ran away. But no one noticed me, not even the police. I was just part of the scene. Invisible. And I'd soon be a corpse if I didn't get out of there fast.

***

After three unbearable days of wandering, I thought of going to the police station in Ranam – I wanted to try my luck at the orphanage there and I needed authorisation from the police. But they turned me down, saying I was not a child and had no business there. I spent seven days and seven nights on the steps of the police station. On the eighth day, 27 August 2004, the police took pity on me and sent me to the orphanage, all the while reminding me that they were watching me.

The manager of the orphanage reminded me of Seong-ho's friend who had helped me that first night in Rimku, when he unknowingly got me out of that bedroom and welcomed me to the village. The director too had an innate benevolence: he applied a white powder to my leg every day. To this day I don't know what the powder was, but it worked nonetheless.

Two months later, when my wound was more or less healed and I was finally able to get around Ranam, a man came to the orphanage looking for me. Thinking it was one of the police officers who came around regularly to make sure I hadn't tried to escape, I was cold but polite. When he told me discreetly that he could smuggle me into China, my heart stopped. This was my chance: I had to go with this man if I was to get out of Ranam. He had heard that I'd been kicked out of China and offered to help me go back. It took many conversations under the bridge in Ranam for me to be sure he was not a spy. That he was a middleman trying to get rich on the backs of the Korean women he snuck into China was almost a relief. Just like Jogyo in 1998, he would sell me to a Chinese man and take his commission on the sale. I knew the scenario. Just like Jogyo, he would probably take advantage of me, too: such was the price of getting to China.

***

At 2am on 2 November 2004, after two weeks of waiting in Musan, the smuggler, a twenty-three-year-old Korean woman, an old man and I crossed the Tumen River. Once across, we followed narrow mountain paths so as to escape notice by the Chinese police. There were many more of them then than there had been in 1998. The paths made us lose our bearings, and we had to take a taxi to Hwalyong, the town where the middleman lived, all the while knowing that in China taxi drivers were government spies and that it was a very risky move. I chatted in Chinese with the driver, telling him that the smuggler was my husband, that the other North Korean was my mute little sister and that the old man was my father. I told him they were Chinese of Korean descent and that they didn't speak Chinese very well because they had spent their whole lives in the countryside. He believed me and suspected nothing.

We had got to China thanks to the smuggler, but in the end it was I who saved our lives.

It was 9pm when we arrived at the middleman's home. I had scarcely set foot in his flat when I told him about Chul and my desire to find him.

'I can't sell you if you have a child,' he said calmly, lighting a cigarette. 'Go find him yourself.'

I couldn't say a word. Too many emotions. As a father, he understood the pain of being separated from one's child, but he was especially grateful for how I'd handled the taxi driver.

He handed me his phone and said I could call Chul. A number popped into my head straight away – it was the one Seong-ho used when he would call his parents from Harbin in 2003. I hurried to take the phone. The first time I rang, someone picked up, then hung up right away. The second time, I got Seong-ho's mother and I hung up even faster. On the third try, I dared murmur, 'Chul, it's *Umma* ... it's *Umma!*'

On the other end of the line there was silence, followed by a sob. It was Chul. I knew he had recognised me, so I hung up and stopped calling. I had located him, now all I had to do was get him.

***

I succeeded in kidnapping Chul from Seong-ho's house on 18 March 2005, and on 21 March, after spending a few days in Yeonbyeon with a distant relative on my mother's side, he and I left for Beijing. There we joined a group of North Koreans who, like us, wanted to cross the Gobi Desert to get to Ulaanbaatar, where we would seek asylum at the South Korean Embassy.

***

It was so hard to keep my head up as I walked and pretend to be alive …

'Come along, Chul, give me your hand. Don't be afraid, just 200 metres more. See that barbed wire fence? Mongolia is just on the other side. You and I can walk, we don't have to run like the others. Everything's going to work out, you'll see.'

Was it a descent into hell or a race for our lives? Whatever. Our flight had begun.

As the other fugitives sprinted the most important 200 metres of their lives, Chul and I walked steadily onward, he a five-year-old and I, limping along with a tetanised leg. His hand in mine was cold but in his eyes fear had been replaced by confidence. Behind us, the wail of a police siren was sounding more and more threatening. I flashed back to prison camp, to North Korea, to Hell … I told myself that it was out of the question that my son should see me in handcuffs a second time.

Just as I came back to my senses, someone grabbed Chul, threw him over his shoulder and started running for the barbed-wire fence. I ran, too, grabbing this stranger's arm. Did we run for a few seconds? Minutes? An eternity? I couldn't say, but one thing was certain: the barbed wire, the siren and the dust were truly behind us: before us lay Mongolia.

And this man, Kwang-hyun Joo. My child and I had ventured our lives; by risking his life, he had saved ours. Did he know that the 200 metres he had just run were not the end but the beginning? That he had just signed on for a journey of undetermined duration – a lifetime together?

EPILOGUE

North Korea, too, has its love stories.

Jihyun falls in love with the man who saved Chul's life and her own. After attempting to cross the Mongolian Desert and failing at reaching Ulaanbaatar as planned, they return to China and live there for three years. Soon after their son Yoo-jang was born, they meet an American missionary who leads them to the Office of the United Nations in Beijing.

On 28 January 2008, Kwang-hyun Joo, Chul, Jihyun and Yoo-jang land at London Heathrow in the United Kingdom, where they are granted political refugee status.

They settle in Bury, a town near Manchester. Chul attends a prestigious university in London. Yoo-jang and Yoo-jin are both known in their respective schools for being good at maths – just like their older half-brother, Chul. Just like their mother.

Jihyun begins taking English language classes at night. Two years later, in 2010, she earns her General Certificate of Secondary Education. It's then that she begins her human rights work. In 2014, she officially becomes an activist.

In 2015, Amnesty International is making a film about Jihyun's life. It's during the filming of the documentary that I meet her.

***

To this day, Jihyun has had no news of her family. She doesn't even know if her mother is still alive. All she knows is that her mother – like Jihyun herself – was sold to a man in China. When *Eomeoni* left her husband and children under the guise of going to China to make some money, she was probably already a slave. The fact remains that for her whole life Jihyun has felt abandoned by her.

She doesn't know what has become of her brother, Jeong-ho.

She has never had any contact with her sister or her niece.

Her brother-in-law, Sang-chul, became gravely ill. He remains in North Korea to this day.

The farewell letter Jihyun wrote to her father which appears in Chapter Eleven is a letter she has always carried inside her, one that wrote itself upon her heart as she thought about him all those years. She will never forgive herself for leaving him behind.

***

A year after our first meeting, when I went to visit Jihyun in Manchester, her husband handed me a bunch of chives that he had just picked from the garden. Damp earth still clung to the roots. *This feels so familiar*, I said to myself. For me, this feeling was a matter of *Jung* – a concept I'm never able to define when my Western friends ask me its meaning. I tell them that *Jung* is a combination of friendship, attachment, nostalgia, tenderness and generosity, but I'm never satisfied by that explanation. It's more like a kind of intimacy you feel for another person, a feeling so strong that you can't bear to let the other leave without giving him a piece of yourself. *Jung* passes between two people as soon as they establish a personal relationship – even two people who to all appearances have nothing in common, provided they share a common heritage.

Seen from the outside, North Korea is a black box. No one really knows what happens in that place – except for those who have lived there.

Through Jihyun's eyes, I have discovered that country from the inside. I have tried to capture this friction between *imagining* North Korea and *experiencing* North Korea. A girl who is loyal to the fatherland but too poor to feed her father. A model student who allows herself to be brainwashed for a good part of her life but who, once she switches sides and becomes a teacher, comes to understand just how corrupt the system is. A woman who is betrayed by her mother and sister but who would forgive them their sin in exchange for a sign of life.

In telling this story, I have tried to untangle these contradictions one by one and share what I have learned, writing the history of the two Koreas alongside the story of two Koreans – two women who are proof that in the North and in the South, beyond the obvious incongruities lies a deep desire for reunification.

POSTSCRIPT

Life in the UK

Our story, unfinished, stops here, in the middle of the Gobi Desert. The threat of death is right before us while survival hovers on the horizon like a mirage. As people's lives vanish beneath the sands, we readers prepare to close our book.

While the launch of North Korean ballistic missiles in 2017 pushed me to take up my pen, four years later, on 25 March 2021, the launch of more ballistic missiles gave me an opportunity to question my writing/work and the progress of my thinking.

We are right back where we started. Efforts at diplomacy carried out on the global stage have yielded nothing and the pit separating North from South Korea has been dug a little deeper. Between the threat of war resurfacing and a seventy-year-long history of being divided, I would have every reason to cry were it not for the news that has occupied the front pages of the British papers these past few months.

The headlines tell of a former teacher who fled North Korea and eventually sought refuge in the United Kingdom – and who is seeking election as a member of Prime Minister Boris Johnson's Conservative Party. As the first North Korean refugee to stand in local elections in Bury, a city in northern England, this woman will go down in the history books of British politics if she wins her seat: her name is Jihyun Park.

This solemn-faced woman whom I feel I know so well and who continues to surprise me on a daily basis radiates an intense strength. Within her she carries the weighty and the insignificant, the past, the present. Jihyun, this unlikely candidate, reveals to me how she recently went from being a refugee who did not even speak English to joining the political ranks.

'I have never forgotten the kindness of strangers,' she tells me.

The man who tended to her leg as she lay dying on the pavement after leaving a labour camp in North Korea; the Korean-American minister who placed her under the protection of the United Nations in Beijing so that she might make it safely to the UK; the owner of a South Korean restaurant in Manchester where she worked as a waitress, who gave her free snacks for her children; but above all, the English people, be they staff in the Home Office, members of the group Action Refugees who set her up in her first temporary housing, the Bury Regional Council, or her next-door neighbours – all these people welcomed her with open arms when she arrived in the UK.

Her arrival at London Heathrow with her husband and two children on 25 January 2008 went seamlessly. The airport officials saw to their needs and the family went through immigration without a hitch, almost certainly thanks to a letter that the Beijing office of the UN had given Jihyun. She didn't know what the letter said but understood that six words which appeared at the beginning of the letter – 'I don't speak English' and 'North Korea' – were working miracles.

The day after arriving in London, Jihyun was at the Liverpool branch of the Home Office (or UK Visas and Immigration Liverpool Premium Service Centre) when it opened. She and her family had spent the night on a bus they had boarded at Victoria station in London. They were all drunk with fatigue, but hopes of a new life in their host country gave them the strength to hold on. Jihyun said

'North Korea' – the only two English words she knew – to the first clerk who appeared. Once again, an entire team began fussing over her as though she'd just given them a hugely important mission. It took an entire day for them to be photographed, interviewed and fingerprinted, but it was worth the wait: each member of the family came away with an Asylum Seeker card. This would serve as their proof of ID until they obtained their refugee visas in the months to come.

On 28 October 2008, after moving house among several temporary residences in Liverpool and Manchester, Jihyun finally was able to move into permanent housing in Bury, which the municipal authority assigned to her. It was a house devoid of human warmth, one without carpeting or furniture that had been left to gather dust, but it was her house – her very own. The thought made her happy. She had a roof over her head, hot water, electricity. She'd receive financial assistance from the UK government twice a month until she found a job. Her children enrolled at the local English school. Her husband, who suffered from heart trouble as a result of the torture he'd endured in North Korea, received continuous care from the National Health Service. And then, in December 2008, almost a year after arriving in the UK, Jihyun gave birth to a third baby, the first and only child of hers to have a birth certificate. The other two, both of them born in China, had never been recognised by the Chinese government and have only officially existed on paper since arriving in Britain.

Koreans are rarely the first to speak up. Jihyun is one of those people who speaks little and doesn't like to open up about herself. She imagined living a quiet little life with her husband and children in Bury. Even back in 2012, when her son had put her back to the wall by asking a question that turned her life upside down, she still kept silent all those years.

Over time, thanks to a friend who invited Jihyun to attend university classes with her, she took English lessons and discovered the Rights of Man. On 23 October 2013, she testified in front of the UN's Human Rights Council. She began helping undocumented

North Koreans in the UK by putting them in contact with solicitors. She set about teaching English to North Korean refugees and taught [North] Korean to English students at the prestigious SOAS University of London.

Her words have taken a while to ripen, but they're beginning to come out. Jihyun talks about her fellow North Koreans who have not managed to leave the country, mothers who, like her, have had to 'abandon' their families without wanting to. When invited to be a guest lecturer at British universities and international organisations, she broadcasts their pain. At the 2018 Asian Women of Achievement Awards, she received the Chairman's Award; that same year, she made The Times' Alternative Rich List. In 2020, she received an Amnesty Brave Award from Amnesty International UK.

Koreans are rarely the first to speak up.

I, too, have always been quiet. How many times did I hear my teachers at French lycée say to my father, 'Sir, your daughter is overly timid. She needs to speak up more in class.' Being an introvert was a handicap, especially in Western culture which tends to reward those who speak loudly, and yet my father's rejoinder saved me: 'Madame Professor, silence is an undisputed virtue in Asian culture. I would not want my daughter to change for anything in the world!'

That phrase was like the stroke of a magic wand. There was no harm in being the pupil the natural sciences professor didn't like. The key was not to allow myself to be defined by the judgement of others and therein lay the power of my father's phrase: silence could be a strength. It was all a question of perspective. Since then, that shy girl of twelve has never lost her bearings.

They say adventures never end. This adventure is ongoing, and writing this book thrusts me into the limelight, enabling me to do things I'd never imagined myself capable of doing. On 25 January 2020, with the support of the National Unification Advisory Council, an entity of the South Korean government which is represented in Britain, I organise a huge Lunar New Year celebration for seventy North Koreans and seventy South Koreans living in the UK.

Amid the Korean language, music and food, we are caught up in a whirl of laughter, tears, dancing and singing that leaves us dazed with the happiness of simply being Koreans together for an evening. I begin to understand that I must open the world's eyes to these signs of happiness which otherwise will go unnoticed – I must document the micro-reunification which is taking place in the heart of the UK.

A year later, on 11 March 2021, Jihyun and I co-teach an online course to some forty French students studying Korean civilisation at the University of Paris. I speak French and Jihyun English, while the students ask questions in Korean. My computer screen captures in real time poignant reactions, including the fascination in the participants' expressions, and becomes a mosaic of faces which condenses wonderfully well the intense feelings into a compact little rectangle. The mixture of languages and cultures moves me to tears. Here again is that particular phenomenon of feeling comfortable between borders which I mentioned at the beginning of this book.

When walls come down, people come together. Within each of us is that innermost space, the 'homeland/native home that everyone carries within himself,' as Milan Kundera writes in his novel *Ignorance*, and where the mysteries of human creation are at work. Peace does not emerge from a North Korea/South Korea summit meeting but from that intimate place of personal interactions, bits of conversation that nurture the desire to be together, the melancholy of a history shared, a childhood lost.

As she readies her campaign in the Moorside electoral district of Bury, Jihyun also plunges into her most personal memories. She thinks about her father. The love he expressed for her was the foundation on which she had built her life, the source from which she'd drawn the strength needed to run in a regional election even though she was 'merely' a political refugee. In one interview, she is asked why she wants to become town councillor and she replies simply that she is deeply grateful to the British government for having given her a second life and that she in turn wants to give back by working for the good of her community.

Jihyun illustrates her point by evoking her experience during the health crisis of 2020. She can't bear to see so many deaths brought about by the coronavirus in Manchester. The suffering of her loved ones and neighbours reminds her of the horrors of famine in North Korea in the nineties. At the time, she had been powerless in the face of human suffering. Seeing the UK in a state of distress, she understands the pain. She comes to serve as the soul of Moorside and leads a counter-attack on the virus in her own small way. In June 2020, she hands out masks that a North Korean refugee living in South Korea has sent her. She goes door to door round the neighbourhood and even reaches out to retirement homes. In the grand scheme of things, 1,000 masks are not a lot but for her community it was an unbelievable feat.

Reading the words of thanks which she received from neighbours and retirement home health workers, something inside her clicks: Britain needs her. The moment has come for her to help the country which so warmly welcomed her. Her moment has come. Why the Conservative Party?

'Don't speak to me of Socialism! Justice, freedom and the family, these are the values I believe in!' she tells me.

Go all the way back to your childhood if you have to. Search your heart until you find the magic phrase that your parent or grandparent or loved one whispered to you, the phrase that made you who you are today, the phrase that gave you strength and made you believe you have the power to change the world.

In looking at Korea in a new light, Jihyun and I have unmuted ourselves. With our voices, we have taken up the call. In tandem. In tune. Our voices travel at the speed of sound. The action each of us takes leaves a mark on the other. We are establishing a new relationship to the world through literature.

Let us not forget that we have the good fortune of living in a free and democratic country – and in return, let us be clear about what we want to do with this freedom and this democracy.

ACKNOWLEDGEMENTS

Jihyun Park

Writing this book has been a search for complete contentment. I have looked back on the events that drove me to the threshold of death and realised that my life is precious. Every moment is a basket of happiness for me.

I would like to thank Seh-lynn, who wrote this book with me. We can't see the dark shadows in the minds of others, and sometimes we don't even try. However, Seh-lynn is a true free spirit. She approached me first, comforted my heart, and brought me a smile once again.

Michael Glendining and James Burt became my first friends and colleagues when I arrived in an unfamiliar place, in England, and did not know the language or culture. They are my role models and are still my friends.

I would also like to thank my neighbours who welcomed the unknown refugee family into their community and always greet me with a sincere smile, as well as the local residents of Bury, Greater Manchester; the local Conservative Party of Bury; and the staff of Bury Town Hall.

Among the people who made me who I am today, there is my father, who is my eternal role model. Had it not been for his courageous decision, I would not have been able to get out of the dark cave of hell forever, and I would not have known what freedom and happiness were now.

And because of my children, Yong-joon, Yoo-jang and Yoo-jin, who have always been a source of love and support, I can always walk proudly today.

Finally, my greatest gift is my true companion and husband, Kwang-Hyun Joo. Without him, I might still live with regret at having been born a woman. He was the first person to let me know that being a woman was something to be proud of and to let me know that my pain is someone else's. He told me that I deserve to be loved. He taught me that happiness is not subtracted, but added, and that we not only have the right to be happy, but that we also have a duty to make others happy.

I'm not religious, but every day I ask, 'Why did you save me and why did you send me here?'

I hope this book begins to answer those questions.

Seh-lynn Chai

I would like to offer my heartfelt thanks to my parents, my brother and my sister for giving me their blessing to write and publish this book.

I am particularly grateful to my father, a career diplomat par excellence, who served his country for fifty years and embodied the love of our country with an extraordinary sense of duty and devotion; I would like to show my profound admiration for my mother, who raised her three children in Africa, and who gave us a taste for kimchi made of cabbage from her garden. Their sense of diligence and dedication made me who I am today.

I would like to express my appreciation to Vera Michalski, who had faith in me and agreed to publish the original book in French; I would also like to thank Mikyung Lee and Sangmi Jang for their hard work in making the Korean version possible.

I would like to show my gratitude to my friends Alexandra and Daniel Pinto, who supported my work faithfully over the years and introduced me to our translator, Sarah Baldwin-Beneich, as well as our literary agent, Caroline Michel.

This book also immensely benefited from the support of Fleur Pellerin, Isabelle Autissier, Jean-Paul Paddack, Ambassador Enna Park, Rosie Whitehouse, Dominique Pourtau-Darriet and the members of Atelier Ecriture, Laure Capel-Dunn, Claudia Lahaie, Diane Frost, Florence de Haut de Sigy, Isabelle Haynes, Sandra Arditti, Corinne Lejeune and Christelle Flinois, whose encouragement and input were indispensable in the making of the book.

Finally, I would like to thank Jihyun Park, who, by sharing her story, helped me find my place in this world.

BOOK CREDITS

HarperNorth would like to thank the following staff and contributors for their involvement in making this book a reality:

Hannah Avery
Fionnuala Barrett
Claire Boal
Peter Borcsok
Charlotte Brown
Sarah Burke
Alan Cracknell
Aya Daghem
Jonathan de Peyer
Anna Derkacz
Jane Donovan
Tom Dunstan
Kate Elton
Mick Fawcett
Simon Gerratt
Monica Green
Lauren Harris
Megan Jones
Jean-Marie Kelly
Oliver Malcolm
Dan Mogford
Alice Murphy-Pyle
Adam Murray
Genevieve Pegg
Agnes Rigou
James Ryan
Florence Shepherd
Eleanor Slater
Emma Sullivan
Katrina Troy
Phillipa Walker